Social Media Marketing

Instagram, Facebook, Youtube, and Twitter
Advertising Guide for Influencers
By: Gary Clarke

information contained within this document, including, but not limited to, — errors, omissions, or inaccuracies.

Chapter 1

1.0 Determining The Best Direction To Take

You may or may not be aware that the most popular social media platforms in this day and age were not the first to exist on the internet. Even the ones that we are dealing with in this book aren't the oldest. In fact, many platforms that came out before Facebook, Instagram, or Twitter and were equally successful in those eras. For example, SixDegrees.com launched in 1997 and has been considered the first social media website to be created. In the 90s, instant messaging became a fad and blogging started to gain traction as well.

However, social media is indeed a fickle thing. SixDegrees.com became defunct in 2001, only 4 years after it launched. Vine, a popular short video sharing app, was acquired and launched by Twitter in 2013 - only to shut down in 2016. Some platforms get bought out by bigger companies, forcing changes to be enforced (like when Facebook bought Instagram, or Microsoft bought Skype).

The point here is, change will always occur when it comes to social media. For the most part, there is a huge growth as people's curiosities are piqued and everyone wants to give it a try. And then the popularity plateaus as interest wanes and some customers decide that a particular website isn't really up their alley. In some cases, there's then a slow decline.

This definitely makes it difficult for marketers to reach their customers in the best way possible for them. How do you plan your campaign and budget when you have no idea whether this social media platform will still be active over the next few years? How do you keep up with the changes and ongoing trends in the current platforms? Having this kind of foresight is a rare thing in marketing. Nevertheless, you must try to answer those questions if you really want to up your game in reaching potential customers.

Before you even think about marketing on any social media platform, you need to figure out your social voice. This chapter aims to help guide you on where to start in determining the right combination of social platforms on which to launch, sustain, and promote your brand. If you are ready, here we go!

1.1 How to Choose The Right Platform

First of all, you need to understand that as a marketer, you cannot and should not limit yourself to using only one platform. That's the biggest marketing faux pas! You will not be able to maximize your reach with a single platform, as not all your customers use the exact same ones - nor do they use only one. Your customers will have at least two social media profiles and you must ensure you reach them on as many as possible. Furthermore, you have to assume that your consumers will invariably gravitate from one social platform to another as time passes. For example, whereas Facebook may have the greatest scale, the sharp rise in usage of Instagram, Pinterest, Tumblr, and WhatsApp shows how fickle consumers can be.

Additionally, you'll notice that it doesn't cost that much more to market on more than one social media platform. What is important is for you to have a clear focus and strategy across your entire marketing campaign - even if the execution is different for each platform. Using more than one undoubtedly makes sense if doing so allows you to reach a different demographic in different ways at different points in the marketing funnel.

You're probably still wondering where you should then focus your efforts. Given the vast number of platforms out there, it's not really possible (or advisable) to market all of them. Trying to do so may negatively impact your efforts as you may end up neglecting and that will look bad for your brand. Though it may be cheap, you're still going to have to expend time and money to maintain dozens of social media accounts. This can also come with some confusion and dissatisfaction to customers.

The solution here is to focus your marketing efforts on just the few that you know your customers use the most. Then you can have a lighter presence on others that you think might supplement your main marketing campaign.

To start off picking the right platforms to use, you need to take a closer look at your audience. See how you can interact with them and where they are making their purchasing decisions related to your company. For purposes of this discussion, you can break your audience down into the following three groups:

1. **Customers**: Obviously, this is your main target. You want to connect, interact, and prompt them to buy from you. You need to understand why they buy, where they buy, and what influences their purchasing process.

2. **Industry**: These are the people who may be competitors, vendors, governing bodies, and so on. In the social media world, this group helps to support your visibility and influence with media outlets and customers directly, too.

3. **Employees**: They can be either your greatest strength or weakness, depending on how you prepare them to participate in social media. If you don't have staff to dedicate to a project, you have a different kind of problem to solve.

Below is a look at how to work through the issues of picking platforms that support each group.

1.2 Learning About Your Customers

Choose where to practice social media marketing by researching and understanding where your customers are spending most of their time. This does not mean identifying where most of your customers have registered profiles, but instead researching where the customers have the highest levels of engagement. This means the following:

● *Finding out what amount of time they spend on the social platform, what they specifically do, and how they use it to interact with other people.*

Tools like Quantcast (www.quantcast.com) can help you understand engagement, but you may need to reach out to the social platforms themselves to understand the details of the engagement. Keep in mind that with Quantcast, only if the site has been Quantified (which means that the site owner has added Quantcast code to his site) are the statistics the most accurate. comScore (www.comscore.com[1]), on the other hand, is a paid solution that can provide more accurate numbers for non-Quantified sites.

You may also want take a survey of your customers directly to understand their social media usage. There are several good survey tools, including SurveyMonkey (https://www.surveymonkey.com/) and Zoho Survey (https://www.zoho.com/survey/).

---

1.   http://www.comscore.com

● *Understanding the user behaviors on the social platform.*

For example, let's say that you're a business-to-business (B2B) solutions provider. You see that your customers use LinkedIn to ask each other for advice when making business-related purchasing decisions but spend a lot more time on Facebook. In this case, LinkedIn may still be a better place to practice social media marketing since that's where they are making the purchasing decisions that matter to you. It doesn't matter if they're spending more cumulative minutes on Facebook.

In addition, consider monitoring mentions of your brand, competitors, product names, or industry keywords to determine how much activity occurs across the platforms.

Invariably, you discover that three to four social platforms match your customers' demographics, have high engagement levels for them, and are what we loosely call locations of influence as far as your product category is concerned. That's where your customers make their decisions, get influenced by others, and observe how their peers are purchasing or discussing their own purchases. These factors together tell you where to practice social media marketing. And as you do so, recognize that you must also consider two broader aspects:

1) **Watching the macro trends of the social platform.** For example, is the platform an emerging one, has it settled into a plateau, or is it fizzling? Accordingly, you may want to devote more or fewer dollars and effort to it.

2) Determining whether the social platform is a place where your brand will have permission to participate and one in which you will want to participate. Participating in some social platforms may hurt your brand. For example if you are a high end, exclusive brand like Chanel, it may not be appropriate to engage in conversations in a casual, music-oriented social environment like the new version of Myspace.

Your customers move between platforms as time passes. As a result, be prepared to adjust your social media marketing campaign significantly. Your customers may not always stay on the platforms that you're targeting currently. This potential migration matters especially to small business marketers.

Each social network has a reputation. Make sure that your brand is in alignment with that reputation. For example, Tumblr is known to be photocentric and has a reputation for attracting a young, creative user. Keep a platform's reputation in mind as you choose where and how to market.

1.5 Addressing Your Industry Influence

A look at your industry yields a very long list of potential competitors, partners, vendors, and associations for you to connect with. The social media marketing goal is to make this group aware of your influence in the marketplace. There are a lot of tools around social media that are available for your use. With this tools, you can compile and gather information, such as the following:

SOCIAL MENTION (http://socialmention.com/) is a free to access service that allows users to search for information just about anything. All that is required of you is for you to type in the name of your company and it searches over a hundred social media properties to streamline all the information you would need. This includes strength, sentiment, and reach. It even gives you general keywords surrounding your search term.

MARKETING   GRADER (https://website.grader.com/) evaluates the marketing on your website using Hubspot's tool for grading websites. It looks at a variety of measures, including your traffic rank, indexed pages, and linking domains.

FOLLOWERWONK (followerwonk.com) can evaluate your Twitter account and provide a visual depiction of your Twitter feed according to influence, popularity, engagement, and user habits.

You now have a basic idea of what it takes to determine how to best go about social media marketing. It's certainly no walk in the park but if done properly and with due diligence, it should yield the best results possible for your brand. Just remember that it's not about dipping your toes into all the platforms out there! Know your audience and focus your energies on those that work best for them because in the ends, that's also what'll work best for you.

The next few chapters you are about to read will dive deeper into a few of the more popular social media platforms in the industry today. The chapters will also explain how you can utilize these platforms to build your social media marketing campaigns.

Chapter 2

Linkedin

2.0 Introduction

Many years ago, interacting with people was so limited to a specific region and communicating overseas can be a bit of a tremendous job and unlikely to catch the interest of many. Thankfully, when the web was invented, everything became possible as people can now socialize with others abroad by just using their devices every time and anywhere across the globe! You can get to know people that are also connected with your peers.

Linkedin is a little different from other social media platforms that we know like Instagram, Twitter, or Facebook because it focus on the corporate world. It provides details about your most recent or new workplace or new shopping acquisition among many others. The tone is serious and the social media marketing potential is vast because people join the platform to network. If you sell to a business audience of any kind, LinkedIn can provide you with a great focus group of interested members. According to a study done by BtoB magazine in April 2011, 26 percent of B2B marketers cite LinkedIn as their single most important social channel, with 20 percent choosing Facebook, 19 percent citing blogging, and 14 percent citing customer communities.

When LinkedIn (www.linkedin.com) launched in May 2003, many questioned whether it truly fit the mold of a social media networking site. LinkedIn has grown from having 79 million users in March 2011 to 300 million in May 2014. That's tremendous growth!

Why did LinkedIn grow so robustly? Like all the other popular social networks, it met a need. It provided a way for like-minded business people from around the globe to find each other, share information, and give advice. It legitimized a way for professionals to communicate in an environment that had guidelines and accountability.

The key to success is remembering that LinkedIn is just one channel of your social media strategy. You need to pay attention to how your connections here can drive traffic to other social media platforms. For example, you may want to provide a link to a discount on your website. By integrating selling with everything else you're doing, you won't seem like a crass self-promoter.

In this chapter, we look at LinkedIn's varied uses for social marketing of both yourself and your company, starting off with the basics: how to get started? From there, we'll talk about how you can use the strong profile you've built to expand your network using the LinkedIn groups. As a bonus, the latter part of the chapter covers how you can market yourself *as an individual.*

2.1 Setting Up Shop on LinkedIn

You can look at the marketing potential of LinkedIn in two ways: First, as a tool to help out your own career as an individual. Second, as a tool to understand your audience better in order to interact with and market to them more appropriately as a company.

Considering the way LinkedIn is structured, you can assume that everyone on it is open to the idea of networking. After all, LinkedIn is primarily for networking and the members understand that any connection made on the website is valuable. However, this also means that you can't be too frivolous when making connections on LinkedIn. At no time should you connect with someone without the understanding that you or your contacts could also be of value to them.

Going back to getting started, LinkedIn gives you the option to start with a free account which you can always upgrade later on if you feel the need to do so. The free account already has tons of free features, so you can use this to explore and get a feel of the platform first. If you decide later on that it'll be worth it to make a financial commitment, then you're welcome to upgrade your account.

If you've already been using LinkedIn and want to get started on using it to build your brand right away, then jump right into LinkedIn Premium.

2.2 What's in the premium subscription?

A few of the most useful features are:

InMail: This premium feature allows you to email anyone on LinkedIn regardless of whether that person is in your network or not, although you are restricted to a certain number of emails. A free account lets you access only your immediate network. Note: If you do not get a response from the person to whom you sent the email, that user is not counted toward your monthly limit. The Business premium account allows three InMails per month; the Business Plus premium account allows 10 InMails per month; the Executive premium account allows 25 InMails per month.

More access to profiles and people when you search: A premium account allows you to see more profiles than you would if you have a free account. This access to more profiles increases the likelihood that you will find the right person to connect with.

Search filters: You can apply a variety of filters to your search so that you can zero in on the right target. For example, you can search for people who work for a certain size company or target only the Fortune 1000.

Expanded profiles: When you see profiles, you see a more expanded profile of the people in which you are interested. You also see everyone on LinkedIn who fits the criteria, not just those limited to your own network.

Who Viewed My Profile: This feature of the free account allows you to see who viewed your profile. The list is restricted to a few names and profiles. However, with a premium account, you can see *everyone* who is interested in you and how each person found you.

With all of these additional premium features, you're probably asking yourself: how much will all of this cost you? You have the following payment options[1]:

- Business: This is the first tier. If you choose to prepay for the annual subscription, it is $287.88 (at the rate of $23.99 per month). The monthly rate is $29.99.

- Business Plus: At this tier, you prepay $575.88 annually (at the rate of $47.99per month). The monthly rate is $59.99.

- Executive: At the highest tier, you prepay $899.88 annually (at the rate of $74.99 per month). The monthly rate is $99.99.

To see the number of users you can access using specific features at each tier, c the subscription chart on the LinkedIn website.

If you are more than a casual user of LinkedIn, you may want to try a premium account. The premium levels specifically for job seekers are discussed later in this chapter, in the section "Finding a Job."

2.3 Creating a new LinkedIn profile

Regardless of whether you're using it for personal career goals or consumer research, the general tone of any interaction will definitely be formal and professional. Therefore, you need to look over your general business strategy to see which of your goals can be propagated on LinkedIn.

After figuring that out, you need to move a step forward to finding out the best way to present yourself to your potential connections. To do this, you need to set up your profile. Now, you can only set up one profile so you need to make sure that it suits all of your needs.

You could opt to set up a company page from the outset, but we don't really advise that you do that right away. We recommend that you wait until you're more familiar with LinkedIn to do this - unless you're setting up a page with several employees already. It's just better to be able to navigate the platform expertly in case you make a mistake.

Setting up a LinkedIn profile is really easy - it just takes some work. It's better to spend more time on making an account so that you can give as many details as possible - quality is the most important part of your profile. Considering it's a professional activity, anyone who looks into you and your company will be judging you on a number of things, including previous achievements and successes, as well as your knowledge on specific subject matter.

We also recommend that you start building your profile around the main goals of your marketing campaign. After that, you revise it as you go along to support more details. For example, if you're looking for a job, your profile will have different content from that of a business owner doing market research. We cover these differences in the rest of the chapter.

2.4 Preparing a Content Strategy

You've probably heard a good deal about the concept of content strategy. It boils down to evaluating what content you have and what you need to meet a specific marketing goal. Content can be articles, product descriptions, videos, audio interviews, or any material that informs people about you or your business.

To illustrate, one of your LinkedIn goals might be to find new consulting clients. If this is the case, you want to review all the content you have created that shows off your consulting expertise. Then you can start to share it on your profile. Afterwards, you can use this newly repurposed content on other platforms, such as your newsletter or blog.

Begin by doing an inventory of your e-books, posts, proposals, and so on, and determine what content you can use to let colleagues learn about you on LinkedIn. Then make an editorial schedule for yourself so that you can create in a timely manner any new items you need. Usually if you don't schedule a specific time to do this, you may end up not doing it. For inspiration, look at other people's profiles and see what they have posted.

2.5 Covering What Matters First

Your profile continues to evolve as you meet new people, join more groups, and attend events. You can't do everything all at once. Consider the following tips when you are starting out:

1. **Keywords matter.**

We made keywords the focal point and first one on the list of what we are discussing. This is necessary because as you put together your profile, you will want to make sure that you include keywords that can be used to find you. You probably have some keywords that you already use for your websites and other channels. Make sure to include some of those, but also think through the goal of this profile and include any new keywords that will move you toward the top of the search results.

1. **List the professional name you wish to be known by.**

This is the name you use in your industry. You want colleagues and potential connections to find you. Don't use a nickname unless you use it professionally.

LinkedIn lets you create only one profile, so if you own a business, decide ahead of time whether you intend to use your own name or your business name. We recommend that you use your own name in case you close your business or want to change direction.

1. **Use a real headline, not just a title**.

This section introduces your brand. If someone were to give you a wonderful introduction, it would include this content. If you are a bestselling author or award-winning salesperson, or have some special designation, this is the right place to use it (for example: Jane Smith, Award-Winning Salesperson).

1. **Provide a summary that highlights your uniqueness**.

Here you detail the contents of your headline. Think of this as the follow-up to the headline. Imagine that you are speaking right after the person who introduced you. Explain who you are and what makes you different among a sea of other members. Don't be modest - the point here is to really sell and market yourself!

1. **Think carefully about how you list your positions — current and past**:

Display what you are doing now and any significant positions you previously held. This is not a detailed résumé. If you are seeking a new job, see the section later in this chapter called "Finding a Job."

1. **Supply a professional photo**.

This is a key item on LinkedIn. People don't like to admit it because they like to be able to picture the person with whom they're connecting. It's not a beauty contest. Get a professional photo with appropriate attire. Save the pose with your favorite pooch for Facebook.

1. **Use links other than just websites.**

Don't be too literal. You can put in any link that you want to send people to. It doesn't have to be your main website. Just make sure that any link you provide are relevant and polish your brand.

1. **Look at the ways in which you can list your achievements.**

The possible sections available include Education, Certifications, Patents, Languages, Honors and Awards, Organizations, Projects, and Publications and Test Scores. Use any of these that are pertinent. You have wide latitude here to really showcase your talents. Again, make sure you sell yourself.

1. **Ask for recommendations.**

LinkedIn provides a recommendations tool that you can use to solicit comments from people who you may have worked with in the past or present and have been impressed by you. This could include a coworker, manager, or client. Obviously, you want to have great recommendations but don't go crazy at the start. Perfunctory recommendations from your friends aren't all that valuable. If someone has some real value to add, ask for their recommendation when you get started. This section will grow organically because your colleagues want to commend you (and have you commend them) for a job well done.

To make it easier for other LinkedIn members to endorse you, make sure to add a list of skills that you want to highlight in the Skills section of your profile. When other members look at the list, they can pick from skills that you want them to endorse instead of inventing them.

1. **Start making connections**.

Connections are at the heart of LinkedIn's success. You are here to build your network. Remember that these connections are people who will help you reach your goals, so make them meaningful. Don't be in a race to see how many connections you can get. After you reach 500 connections, LinkedIn will only lists your connections as 500+. See more details in "Finding Connections," later in this chapter.

1. **Show work samples**.

LinkedIn has added the ability for you to add your work samples to your profile. Content types include video, images, podcasts, and so on. You should take advantage of this feature when you get started. This way you can highlight your best work up front. You can add samples in the Summary, Education, and Experience sections. This function replaces the built-in app section.

2.6 Accessing LinkedIn from your mobile devices

Of course, you'll want to stay connected when you're on the go if you're searching for a job using LinkedIn. LinkedIn makes it easy to access your connections from your smartphones and mobile devices. You'll find free apps for the following:

- Iphone
- Ipad
- Blackberry
- Android
- Windows

2.6.1 Finding connections

LinkedIn helps you easily get started in finding new connections. One way to start is to click the Connections tab and then click Add Connections. You have several options to choose from. You can find colleagues from your various email programs such as Outlook, classmates from your educational institutions, or people you may know from nonprofits or clubs.

As you are presented with lists of these contacts, go through and choose the ones you want. Be certain to deselect the 'Share All' checkbox so that you do not send invitations to people who don't belong in your network but are on your email lists.

It's really that simple! Growing your professional network has probably never been this easy. You have now gotten your profile set up and have a good understanding of how LinkedIn works. Let's move on to how you can use this platform for your social media marketing campaigns and build your network.

2.6.2 Choosing to Advertise

In contrast to some other social media platforms, advertising on LinkedIn involves little controversy. Perhaps LinkedIn's business orientation keeps the idea of advertising from seeming intrusive. When you are on the site, you find ads on the following pages: Home, Profile, Inbox, Search Results, and Groups.

It's important to know who exactly you're targeting on LinkedIn because the platform makes it very easy for you to separate your ad targets. You can segment your audience into the following groups:

- **Industry:** You can choose a variety of industries applicable worldwide. On LinkedIn, Zoomsphere.com reports that the top five industries are Higher Education (18.7%), Information Technology and Services (13.9%), Financial Services (11.6%), Retail (10.9%), and Computer Software (8.9%).

- **Seniority:** This refers to job seniority, or a person's position in their company. 2 million users on LinkedIn identify themselves as members of C-suite jobs (i.e. jobs with a C in the title, like CEO, CTO, CFO, or COO).

- **Geography:** You can target your audience based on where they are either by region, continent, or country. The United States makes up the largest demographic on LinkedIn with over 27% of users.

- **Job function:** These include Sales, Management, Business Development, Information Technology, and Marketing.

- **Age**: In the United States, 41 percent of the members are between the ages of 35 and 54.

As soon as you have a better understanding of your audience and customers, you can then determine which of the above subgroups you can target such that you get the best results from.

2.6.3 Participating in LinkedIn Groups

Many LinkedIn users don't fully understand the usefulness and value of joining or participating in groups. That's probably because they see the platform as only a medium to find or further their personal careers. People probably forget that it's possible to reach out to your connections' connections to expand your network for whatever reason you need. Joining a group on LinkedIn goes even further beyond that, as you can meet people that you really never would have met in person.

2.6.4 Benefits of Joining Groups

There are many ways that you can get started in LinkedIn groups. One strategy is to join several groups in order to gain as many contacts with similar interests as possible. Another is to simply join one, see how you like it, and then expand your groups from there. You are allowed to join a total of 50 groups, so you can always take your time to decide which of the groups will help you achieve your marketing goals.

Below are some benefits you can get from joining groups:

- **Finding members with similar experiences**. This can include people who work or worked in the same company, or went to the same school as you.

- **Expanding your knowledge of a company in which you are interested**. If you're thinking about working for or partnering with a particular company, you can find other employees to connect with.

- **Connecting with members who are interested in the same activities**. Nonprofit and charitable groups are in abundance. You can find like-minded members easily.

- **Establishing yourself as an expert in your field**: You can choose to take a leadership role in a group or make your feelings known about certain discussion topics.

● **Understanding the trends in your industry**: You can stay informed about important issues and developments.

● **Determining who the industry leaders are**: By virtue of their popularity and activities, you can learn from industry leaders who are active.

● **Connecting with and participating in discussions**: You can do a lot of consumer research in these groups if you take the time to read and listen.

● **Finding partners for joint venture activities**: If you're looking for investors, you may want to extend your feelers out in the group without having to give away too much information.

● **Discovering new clients**: People who are impressed with your breadth of knowledge on a topic can seek you out for consultation.

2.6.5 Starting your own group

If you have determined that starting your own group will better help you meet your business goals, you'll be happy to know that LinkedIn provides a great framework for you to do so. The most important thing to consider before starting is whether you have the time and enthusiasm to be the leader. Managing a group takes work. If you start a group and then let it falter, it reflects badly on your professionalism. With more than 300 million people as potential members, you can develop a solid group fairly quickly but it's your responsibility to keep it lively and active.

Imagine yourself as the host of a party that needs your attention to be a success. This is particularly true for small business owners who wear all the hats in their organization. Picture yourself running this group a year from now and see how that fits into your plans.

Rather than hope that everyone will police their own groups, LinkedIn has set some guidelines. They include the following:

1. **You can send only one email a week to members of your group**.

   You can envision the amount of email that could be generated by a group leader eager to connect (and sell things) to his members. Limiting email communications helps everyone control the information flow and that's actually cool.

1. **The group must either be open or closed (by invitation only).**

You can choose to have an invitation-only group or an open one. If you choose a closed group, members must be approved by the group leader. The members so approved are the only ones who can see and participate in discussions.

If you choose to have an open group, anyone can join. You should be aware that the discussions generated in an open group can be seen by anyone on LinkedIn, not just group members. In addition, the content can be shared on Facebook and Twitter. Leaders of open groups can decide whether everyone on LinkedIn can participate in discussions or just be able to view them.

The group leader can allow members to invite people to join the group. As the group leader, you can allow members to seek out new members for the group by sending them invitations. If they accept an invitation from another member, they are instantly accepted.

2.6.6 Leading a successful group

What are the components of a highly-reputable group on Linkedin? You can build a successful business connection in this social media site. This is obviously what you can achieve by socializing with people effectively as part of a community. Below are the techniques that you can do for you to have a successful group in Linkedin:

1. **Use your weekly email**

    You are allowed to send only one email a week, so make it count. Think of it as the newsletter you might send to your website mailing list. Provide value and help members discover each other.

1. **Hold the line on promotions**

    As the leader, you are responsible for making sure that other members are not over-promoting and ruining the experience. Nothing is worse than feeling like you're being taken advantage of by other group members.

1. **Encourage discussions**

    The discourse in the groups are a valuable part of your content - both for you and your consumers. You'll be able to understand your audience better based on what they know or don't know. On the other hand, your customers will gain more information based on other users' experience.

1.   Use events

As I have said a while ago, LinkedIn has a very functional tool that can be used in events. You can produce several virtual events wherein members can interact with one another. You can get everyone active about upcoming events. If you have caught the attention of a lot of people then you can start an in-person conference.

1.   Catch the Attention of the Media

One of the assignments you need to pursue for your group is to ensure that you gain visibility from the media. This is essential because a highly visible group will do a lot of wonders for your group to become popular. You can have an idea of producing an eBook or other digital products about your niche and give the privilege for the media to get a grasp of it.

2.6.7 Using LinkedIn to answer questions

For you to transform yourself into an outstanding leader on LinkedIn, it is really great to disseminate advice to people. The people who utilize LinkedIn put up some inquiries that needs some professional help. Letting others know your field of specialization is an excellent resort to give a function and it will eventually lead to people noticing you.

One of the greatest ways to give help is with the use of LinkedIn Answers, however, the feature is already not available as it was removed several months ago. Based on LinkedIn, the most effective resort to disseminate your specialization is by using the following features:

- Your LinkedIn Home page
- LinkedIn discussion groups
- Partner sites
- LinkedIn Pulse

LinkedIn Pulse is a news feed gathered by LinkedIn that can be accessed by going to Interests*Pulse in the main menu of your profile. Here you will find news based on your interests as determined by your LinkedIn preferences. In addition, you will see a link to Top Posts on the service and a 'Discover link' that displays suggested people you may want to follow.

Answering questions has an extra function to people that are marketing with the use of social media. For an instance, you can acquire the corresponding benefits:

- **Discovering content for blog posts, e-books, and slideshows**: The greatest resort to produce content is by answering queries. It will also enhance the content that people have are interested in and at the same time you can help a lot of people. If they are not clear to other people, then you can still use it to your advantage by making an additional post regarding it with the use of different media.

- **Uncovering trends by mining the questions people are asking**: If you have seen a latest innovation that is formed, you may have discovered the latest trend. Always be vigilant!

- **Searching for a prospect business partner**: If you are looking for an expert in a particular area, you can ask questions to find other thought leaders who may want to partner with you (or invest).

- **Finding a technical expert**: Locating a technical expert who you understand and trust can be a herculean task. If you find someone who answers your technical questions and can act as a freelancer or consultant, you have saved yourself a lot of time, energy, and money.

- **Letting new clients find you**: A great by-product of showing off your skills is that someone with a budget to buy your products or hire you could be listening. Be generous with your expertise and let people get to know you. They'll be more likely to consider working with you.

2.6.8 Finding A Job

It is now common to have a LinkedIn account if you are trying to look for a job. For basic use, there is no payment required and the good thing is that employers are always online to look for new people that they can hire. However, you must have an excellent-looking profile, build significant amount of contacts, and have fundamentals when it comes to different groups that are related with your niche. Below are tips for you to get noticed by employers:

1. **View your profile from the perspective of an employer**

Place yourself in the shoes of a business as you investigate your profile. On the off chance that a genuine list of qualifications style is required, you can look at Resume Builder at http://resume.linkedinlabs.com. This application encourages you to take your profile and fabricate a gorgeous resume from it, however LinkedIn likewise has a worked in highlight that enables you to transform your profile into a list of references. Survey it cautiously to ensure that the sequential request is precise and matches your profile. If you look for a structure work, ensure that you transfer PDFs, pictures, introductions, and any other thing you need to flaunt.

1. **Produce a compelling presentation**

Furthermore, if you create your résumé to make it appear excellent, ensure that it has great presentation.

Programs such as Prezi can be used to develop something unique. You can also link to SlideShare (http://www.slideshare.net) or post a video. It's worth repurposing your best work and showing it off. You need a way to stand out, and this will help.

1. **Reexamine your keywords**

You may have chosen general keywords when you first signed up. Now that you know specifically what type of job you are searching for, add keywords that will help you get found by your preferred employers.

1. **Create a list of companies you would like to work for**

Even if you are not targeting a specific company, making a list of potential companies will help you. Do some research on what jobs they have open and where you might fit in. It will give you ideas about how to improve your profile. If you do have a target list, look for someone in the company who you might be able to approach for discussion.

1. **Target your recommendations**

If you've been reticent about asking for recommendations, now is the time to actively seek out people whose endorsement speaks directly to the job you want. LinkedIn makes adding a recommendation easy, so it's not an onerous request.

1. **Mine your network**

Look at the second- and third-degree contacts in your network and see whether you want to ask for introductions. That's when the power of LinkedIn is really demonstrated. Get started immediately because this could take some time. Not everyone has the same sense of urgency that you do.

1. Include other channel links

Don't forget that there is a whole wide world of other online channels that you are connected to.

Make sure to showcase a website or show that you have an active Twitter following.

1. Consider purchasing Job Seeker Premium services.

LinkedIn provides special subscription premium tiers for job hunters. If you are considering this, you may want to start with a month-to-month subscription to see whether it works for you. If you find that the job hunt is slow, you can always move to an annual subscription. How much will you have to pay for premium job seeker services? You have the following payment options[2]:

- Job Seeker Basic: This is the first tier. If you choose to prepay for the annual subscription, it is $191.88 (or $15.99 per month). You pay $19.99 go from month to month.

- Job Seeker: At this tier, you prepay $287.88 annually (at the rate of $23.99 per month). You pay $29.99 to go from month to month.

Job Seeker Plus: At the highest tier, you prepay $575.88 (at the rate of $47.99 per month). You pay $59.99 to choose a monthly subscription.

A few of the most helpful features included in the premium accounts are as follows:

- **Job Seeker "Premium" Badge**: Your profile has a visual aid next to it. This helps employers quickly spot you. You can choose to display your badge (or not) in Settings, which is the pull-down menu you see when you click your name in the upper right of the home page. The default choice is Off.

- **See real salary information**: You can zero in on your desired level and see real details from employers.

- **InMail**: As mentioned previously in the section "Getting Started," depending on the premium level you choose, you can contact a set number of members directly.

- **Who's Viewed My Profile**: As we noted previously, this feature allows you to see who viewed your profile. With a premium account, you can see everyone who is interested in you and how anyone found you.

- **Job Seekers Group and Webinar**: Here you can get additional support and advice from the community to help you find a job.

The key to finding a job on LinkedIn is to work the power of your network. Not only can you find almost anyone in the industry or companies you target, but you can also market yourself in the best possible light. Remember that recruiters and employers use LinkedIn on a regular basis. If you make the effort, you could be in the right place at the right time.

Given all of this information about how to build a network both for yourself and your brand on LinkedIn, you should be able to jump on the platform with confidence. With LinkedIn, everything is viewed with more professionalism than what is obtainable on other social media platforms. These platforms will be discussed in the succeeding chapters.

Chapter 3

Facebook

3.0 Introduction

No matter which way you look at it, it's highly likely that Facebook will be a great platform that you can use at hand.

Facebook was founded in 2004 and up till this present moment, it has recorded a significant growth having more than 1 billion active users. It is the largest social network in the United States. Of all users with an account on Facebook, more than 48% log in every day.

Statista.com reports that approximately 201 million North Americans are active on Facebook monthly. Given this information, it's pretty safe to assume that a huge percentage of your customers are not only users of the platform, but are on it at any given time.

According to Facebook Chief Operating Officer Sheryl Sandberg, you should be "social by design." By that she means that social media marketing should be a part of everything you do. With this idea in mind, in this chapter we jump into explaining how you can develop marketing strategies. We also discuss how you can use Facebook to grow your audience and engage your customers through Pages, Events, and Ads.

3.1 Looking at Facebook Basics

Choosing how to use internet-based marketing on Facebook can appear to be threatening in light of the fact that so much is going on at one time. The profile page for every substance has a large group of connections, advertisements, posts, etc. Likewise, changes to the stage itself are being made ceaselessly. You may feel that when you see how something functions, it changes, and this can appear to be overpowering. One approach to conquer this feeling of feeling overpowered is to recall the accompanying:

- The gateway to web-based social networking promoting on Facebook is to comprehend that your system is the key.

Together, you and your companions do things online that may influence each other's conduct. Advertisers endeavor to tackle this movement to their very own favorable position. That is the thing that you have to concentrate on. For instance, if a few clients like your item, their companions will see that suggestion and maybe get it, as well. By understanding the interconnectedness of internet-based marketing, particularly on Facebook, you can construct your business.

- *The heart of Facebook is a user's Newsfeed.*

It is easy to forget that the heart of Facebook is not your Facebook page or a user's profile page. Rather, it is the Newsfeed. This is the page that a user sees immediately they log into Facebook. It shows their friends' activities (including potentially your brand's activity). In 2013, Facebook redesigned the newsfeed so that users would have an easier way to show their followers what matters most to them. Some users have complained that the algorithm that supports this redesign (called Edgerank) actually makes it harder for their fans to see their daily content.

Because it's now harder to predict what your users will see, focusing your Facebook marketing efforts on the Newsfeed is extremely important. A lot more users may learn about your company or your product through the Timeline rather than by visiting your particular company page.

- *Using Facebook requires constant experimentation.*

No one right way to market on Facebook exists. Your audience and products are unique. You can follow some best practices but for the most part, you have to determine what works for your specific audience. If you understand this idea going in, you won't have to feel as though you're failing because things are moving slowly at first. Try something and see how it works. Then use feedback and results to point you in the right direction.

- *You have powerful tools at your disposal to enhance all your other channels.*

Facebook gives you tools to link to other channels where you can promote your company or your products. For example, you can link to your blog, your Twitter account, and so on. Provide a link anywhere you have an opportunity. Don't forget to link all your email addresses and newsletters to your Facebook account as well. For example, when people are on your website, make sure that they see a widget for your Twitter account. Go to the link for "Take Twitter with you" at twitter.com to get the widget to link your Twitter account to your website and other social media platforms.

- *Facebook gives you an SEO (search engine optimization) advantage.*

The search engines regard Facebook Connect as very important content. By publishing to your Facebook page, you can see a potential boost in your rankings.

- *You can easily reach local customers.*

With Facebook, you can easily let customers know where you are, and you can choose to include a map. When customers are at your location, they can also choose to let their friends know. Furthermore, you can target specific posts on Facebook to certain customers only.

- *Pay attention to your Timeline.*

Your Timeline is the place where everyone goes to get your updates. Keep things lively! If you publish only once in a while, people are going to lose interest. Make it a point to put a process in place, and use content calendars to manage the frequency and types of postings to the Timeline.

- *The number of Likes you have should not be your only measure of success.*

The number of Likes you have is only one indicator of interest at a particular point in time. You may have lots of Likes and few engaged customers or buyers, or vice versa. Use several measures, including looking at Facebook's own Insights, to see how you are doing. Pay particular attention to Facebook's People Talking About metric. This represents how many people are interacting with you, such as Liking your page, posting on your Timeline, and commenting or sharing your content. You can find it in Facebook Insights.

Facebook is always in the process of evolving its social platform. Besides the guidance we give in the sections that follow, we recommend visiting Inside Facebook (www.insidefacebook.com) and All Facebook (www.allfacebook.com) to keep pace with the evolving marketing opportunities and advertisement formats on the platform.

3.2 Starting With Search

"In the beginning, there was Search." It will always be.

Okay, that's not *exactly* the right phrase, but just as you do with any good investigation into a subject, you may want to start with a search. When you are determining what's already on Facebook and how that relates to your own social media marketing plan, you want to use Facebook Search, which you can find at www.facebook com/search.

You can narrow your search by using the drop-down menu to select the following:

- All Results
- People
- Apps
- Events
- Web Results

By starting with a search, you can get a good understanding of what exists in your product or service category. For example, if your category is productivity, you can enter that search term and get the results. Then you can filter further by using one of the search categories, such as apps.

The idea is to get an understanding of your customers, competit0rs, and Facebook users' way of doing things. We recommend that whenever you want to investigate a question about the Facebook universe, start here.

3.3 Facebook Pages

Facebook has 30 million active small business pages and counting. Think of Facebook pages as company profiles on Facebook. You can set up a page for your brand and encourage others to "Like" it. It doesn't cost anything to create a business page, but it does take time and effort to make the page relevant and worthwhile.

Don't confuse a Facebook page with a personal profile. A personal profile has your name on it and is about you and your friends. A page is devoted to an entity such as a business, charity, or public figure.

The first thing you need to do is decide what type of page it will be. The choices include:

- Local Business or Place
- Company, Organization, or Institution
- Brand or Product
- Artist, Band, or Public Figure
- Entertainment
- Cause or Community

As you can see, you are provided with a variety of options for your business. Getting started should be easy.

After you've selected your category, you need to decide what to add to your page to help it garner attention. If you begin to think like a social media marketer, you want to consider publishing media that includes the following:

- **Posts, including location-based posts**: Ongoing posts that keep your community informed are necessities. Post as often as you can, but keep it relevant.

- **Photo albums**: You can easily add a set of photos to Facebook in the form of an album. You can add up to 200 photos per album and an unlimited number of albums. Make sure to add any pertinent photos of your products, services, staff members, and anything else that will inspire your customers.

- **Multimedia content**: To ensure that you provide a variety of formats, you can link to slides, videos, and podcasts. Remember that your audience likes to be surprised.

- **Twitter feeds and blog posts**: You can easily link your Twitter feed or blog to show up in your status updates using a plug-in. For example, to link your Twitter feed to Facebook, go to this URL: www.facebook.com/twitter/.

- **Event information**. The opportunity to alert your community to your events is priceless. You can also show the location with a map. See the section "Facebook events," later in this chapter, for more information.

- **Coupons and other promotional items**. You can provide printable coupons and contests or giveaways to customers who "Like" your page. Two things to remember here: First, make sure that you take down expired coupons and contest notices. Second, some people may un-Like your page after they print the coupons or enter the contest. Therefore, make sure that you offer a prize that's relevant for the audience you want to attract and provide content that keeps them engaged even when the contest is over.

In March of 2014, Facebook announced that it was rolling out a newly designed layout for Facebook pages that provides users with more options. The designs vary for online and offline businesses.

3.4 Facebook Groups

Facebook groups are set up by users and are used to discuss topics of interest and express their points of view. In order to join a group, you have to be invited by another member. Facebook groups have begun to wane in popularity with the rise of Facebook Pages. Groups are mostly used because they can offer the privacy that Pages cannot. As a brand, it's better for you to have a page than manage a group, which is really designed for user to user interaction only.

You can market directly in the Facebook groups, but you can certainly identify the ones in which your brand is being discussed extensively. In some cases, you may want to observe the conversation, learn from it, and maybe participate as a social media marketing voice when and where appropriate.

3.5 Facebook Events

If you're holding an event for your customers, employees, or business partners, you can promote it on Facebook by listing it as an event. This can be a virtual or physical event supporting your company, its products, special promotions, or milestones. People can be invited to attend the event as you invite them from within Facebook, either on your mobile or computer. Also the event page can include content about your event, your brand, as well as your products and services.

Conferences, product previews, and special promotions are popularly highlighted through Facebook events. After the event is complete, you can share photos and write-ups of the event on the event page.

If the event is a virtual one in real time, you can do a lot to encourage visitors by creating posts that tease about the event beforehand. You can have different types of events, such as an online Q&A session with a guest, or questions about your latest product. People who use Facebook often appreciate the opportunity to stay there to get answers to their questions from their mobile device or computer. They don't have to make a call or log in to another online chat service. If you wish to stream video events in real time on Facebook, you can also use the Facebook live feature.

3.6 Facebook Applications

Creating pages and events that are supported by advertisements and sponsored stories may not be enough. Some companies choose to build applications that can be installed in a user's profile or on a Facebook page. For a branded application to be a success, it must engage users in a meaningful fashion, whether its purpose is utility or entertainment. The most successful applications can take weeks to build and promote within Facebook, so don't expect this to be a simple endeavor.

Popular applications include games, quizzes, badges, calculators, and tools that analyze a person's social graph, which is a mapping of people and how they relate to each other. For example, TripAdvisor's Cities I've Visited application lets you show your friends which cities around the world you've visited. It has been an extremely popular application. For more information on building Facebook applications, visit the Facebook Developers page (http://developers.facebook.com)

For a list of top Facebook applications you can use a marketer, check out the Ignite Visibility article (https://ignitevisibility.com/10-top-facebook-apps-for-marketers/).

3.7 Facebook Connect/Login with Facebook

Facebook Connect has continued to evolve since its introduction in 2008 and is now commonly referred to as Login with Facebook. In a nutshell, when you use an application that allows you to use Login with Facebook, you have the ability to bring your Facebook social graph to a third-party website. In this case, the social graph is composed of your Facebook network. This means that when users log in to those sites with their Facebook credentials, they can see which of their friends have participated on that website in some fashion, whether by commenting, rating, or writing a product review. Whatever the users do is also sent to Facebook and appears in the Newsfeed of all their friends. But the Newsfeed has some lag time, whereas users can instantly see what their friends are up to by looking at the ticker on the right side of the page.

The ticker allows users to share their activity on third-party websites with their friends in Facebook, which inadvertently gives the site more exposure and greater power from a recommendation perspective. For more information about Login with Facebook, visit the Facebook developers' page (developers.facebook.com)

3.8 The Use of Ads on Facebook

Social media marketing on Facebook is as simple as using Facebook Ads. Facebook has seen the value of advertising on its platform and has worked to enhance this aspect over the years with changes such as Facebook Insights. This built-in statistics tool helps marketers to understand and target their audience based on demographics, user interests, and other essential keywords.

When you start advertising on Facebook, you can immediately see the changes in your reach as you further narrow down and filter your criteria. You also have the option to add ways for your users to interact with the ad, including asking viewers to rate the ad or become a fan of the brand on the platform.

You can also have the viewer of your ad see who amongst their friends are fans of or have endorsed your brand in the past. This strategy is a simple but clever way to catch more consumers' attention.

You can buy Facebook Ads on a cost-per-click (CPC) or a cost-per-impression (CPM) basis. These have been very popular with small businesses because it would allow you to settle on a daily budget and just generally don't cost too much.

You should consider using the following Facebook Ad formats:

1. Sponsored stories

Sponsored stories appear with a title, content, and images, and they look and feel like a story. They appear on the right side of the page and may link to a Facebook page or even to your company's website. It is usually recommended that you link to a Facebook page and keep the user within Facebook itself. The sponsored stories are targeted through profile data like the social advertisements and are popular because they're highly visible.

The Newsfeed is what a user first sees when they log into Facebook. The ads appear on the right side (not in the news stream) but are easily noticed.

A variation on the sponsored story is the sponsored video, which functions in a similar fashion. The sponsored videos are popular because they don't require the user to leave the News Feed to view them. You can learn more about these at www.facebook.com/ads/stories.

1. Advertising your apps

If you've spent the time and money to create an app, you'll probably want to advertise it. Facebook has two specific types of ads to target to your app. These ads are designed to encourage app engagement and to increase app installations. To begin the process and see how they are created, check out https://developers.facebook.com/products/ads/.

Chapter 4

Twitter

4.0 Introduction

Scarcely any social platform has had progressively intense development over the most recent couple of years than Twitter, the microblogging administration. Twitter (www.twitter.com) is like a blogging administration, then again, actually you're constrained to 280 characters (extended from the first 140) per message, or tweet. Likewise, just individuals who tail you on Twitter see your tweets in their Twitter course of events. You answer to other individuals' tweets, forward their tweets, or send them direct messages. Every one of your supporters sees your tweets.

Today, Twitter has roughly 326 million dynamic clients around the globe, 69 million of whom are in the United States. A larger number of individuals make accounts on Twitter than they do on some other social platform — 135,000 new clients consistently. Dissimilar to on Facebook, the biggest web-based life platform, Twitter clients are commonly more established. Despite the fact that the absolute number of Twitter clients is not exactly Facebook clients, it is developing so quickly and has such a persuasive client base.

You can market on Twitter using paid and unpaid methods. You can buy specific Twitter ad products that allow you to draw attention to your Twitter account, attach yourself to specific trends, and align with certain keyword searches. Third-party services let you also buy attention by associating with celebrities.

But in a similar fashion to Facebook, marketing on Twitter must start with the basic unpaid tactics. And as you do that, remember that Twitter is most powerful for building and nurturing relationships between people, even more so than Facebook. It's because you're limited to 280 characters. When marketing through Twitter, focus tightly on building the relationships, and everything else will follow. Don't worry too much about pushing messages to the community. But when you have to, there are smart ways to do that via the Twitter ad products that don't hurt your reputation in the community.

In this chapter, we'll start with covering the basics of how to get yourself started on Twitter. From there, we'll discuss how you can go about engaging with the Twitter community for unpaid marketing, and then paid marketing tactics. Lastly, we've got some tips and tricks that we'd love to share with you!

4.1 Figuring Out Twitter

In case you're not quite familiar with Twitter, it's essentially a communication platform that was originally inspired by SMS (short message service, or texting) and Facebook. On it, you publish short tidbits of thought or information (called "tweets") within only 280 characters. These tweets can be viewed by other Twitter users and you can view others' tweets as well. In order to have this reciprocal relationship, you simply need to "follow" each other on the platform. Unlike being Facebook friends, when you follow people on Twitter, they're not automatically made to reciprocate in return.

Another difference between Facebook and Twitter is that on the latter, your profile is open to the public by default. This means that anyone can view your tweets, which is really the ideal for a brand or company. On Facebook, your personal profile is usually only viewable by your friends. Because a majority of tweets are public, the more than 500 million tweets sent daily are a treasure trove of information for marketers to learn how consumers communicate and interact online.

Below are some of the basic actions you can take on Twitter:

- **Mentions**: As a user on Twitter, you can publish tweets as soon as you've signed up. Just type in your tweet and you're on your way. To "mention" another user, you can refer to their account in your tweet by preceding their account name with the @ symbol. For example, to mention the Pepsi Twitter account in a tweet, you would need to type @pepsi. Then when a user clicks the Pepsi handle (@pepsi), they will automatically be taken to the Pepsi Twitter page.

- **Retweets**: Another unique feature of Twitter is the ability to retweet someone else's tweet. Think of this as a Forward button. You can retweet by clicking the Retweet button that's below every tweet in your Twitter feed. If someone has tweeted something interesting and you want to share it with your own followers, the Retweet button is the one to use.

Messages: Through Twitter, you can also send direct messages to specific users. These messages are private and seen only by the Twitter user it's addressed to and not by anyone else. To send a direct message to someone who is already following you, begin your tweet by typing D, and follow that with the @ sign and the person's account name. For example, to send a direct message to John, type D @John followed by the actual message. Direct messaging is useful when you want to communicate directly with a customer in response to something they may have tweeted.

- **Hashtags**: Preceded by a hash (#) mark, the hashtag is used for spontaneous categories by people who want to participate in a conversation around a specific topic. For example, during the Super Bowl, people who want to tweet about the game include

#superbowl in their tweet. Then, whenever people search for or click on #superbowl, they see all the tweets related to the game. Clicking a hashtag allows a user to see all the other tweets related to that category.

● **Photos and videos**: Recently, Twitter has made it easy to attach a photo that can be seen below your tweet. You just need to click the camera icon when typing your tweet. If you want to display a video, it's the exact same process. Currently, Twitter supports videos that are 2 minutes and 20 seconds long or shorter.

4.2 A Twitter handle

Taking ownership of your brand on Twitter is very important. Sign up on Twitter with your brand or company's name as the Twitter handle so that your customers can easily find and recognize you. If no one has used your company's name, you are lucky. Use this account to communicate company or brand news, special promotions, and product offers; you can also respond to questions, and resolve customer service issues.

If you do not immediately take ownership of your company or brand name on Twitter, someone else may do so on your behalf. This could be a competitor, another business with a similar name, a customer, or a fan. If that happens, you'll probably have to spend a lot of time (and maybe money, too) to get back the username. Most Twitter users automatically associate your brand name on Twitter with your company. Many may not realize that the person behind the Twitter account using your company name is not actually from your company - and that could damage your brand's reputation if that user tweets unprofessional, provoking, or controversial statements.

You'll also want to make sure that you're "verified" on Twitter. To be verified means that *you* are the official representative account for the company. Users will be able to see that you're verified if you have a blue check mark next to your name. To get verified, all you need to do is visit the verification form on Twitter when signing up. In some cases, you may be asked to provide official ID and other information for the platform to be able to check that it's really you.

Now, should you follow every person who follows you? It's good Twitter protocol to do so if you're looking to build relationships with lots of people. If your goal is just customer service, don't feel the need to follow everyone.

However, when you do consider following someone, watch out for spam and viruses. Both spam and viruses have made their way onto the Twitter platform, and probably the easiest way to put your account at risk is to follow another account that is then used to send you links to viruses. So when you choose to follow other people, make sure that they're legitimate people and not spambots or virus malware. It's easy enough to do, too - just click on their profile and look at the kind of content they're tweeting. Red flags to look out for are Twitter handles with long, randomized characters, no profile pictures, and senseless tweets that are just links (and don't click on those links!).

4.3 Preparing for Twitter Marketing

What we've discussed so far covers setting up your account and how you can communicate with the rest of the Twitter community. What comes next is how you can now prepare both yourself *and* your account to engage with current and potential customers.

4.3.1 Twitter searches

For anyone looking to market via Twitter, the first step is to monitor the conversations for your company, brand, and product mentions. You want to know *how* people are talking about you. You can set up these searches easily within Twitter itself or by using a separate application like TweekDeck. Make sure to track not just your company's brand but also your competitors' brands. You'll probably learn more from people talking about your competitors than from their conversations about you. You can use the Twitter search engine or one of the real time engines like Social Mention or Twazzup. You could also try TweetBeep, which gives you Twitter alerts via email on an hourly basis - this'll help you stay on top of everything that happens.

The reason for using a platform like Social Mention or Twazzup is that you can find sorted information in real time. When you use Twitter search, you get a deluge of tweets that you have to sort through. The tweets may be current or a bit older. When you use the real time search engines, you get up-to-the-minute tweets that can be sorted by category. These are the best tools to use for real time marketing campaigns.

4.3.2 Responding to tweets

It's not enough to just listen in on the conversations, though. You have to participate in the conversations, too. This means responding to questions directly addressed to your Twitter username, whether the questions are customer service-related or more general. It also means watching your brand mentions and correcting misinformation (although you don't want to appear defensive when you do this because it can backfire), providing helpful advice when and where appropriate, and broadening relationships with the people who are talking about your company.

Part of being a good social voice is allowing your own personality to shine through, which means opening up and being willing to talk about your own life and not just the brand you represent.

But there can be challenges in being personable and open, too. For example, if you're a mass brand with lots of followers on Twitter and lots of people talking about you, you may have a hard time responding to everyone. It can become cumbersome and resource intensive. Worse still, it may make your Twitter account look like a series of individual responses versus being one that balances responses with fresh, original content.

Managing such a situation can be difficult. If your company receives lots of customer service queries, you may set up a separate Twitter handle to manage those. Similarly, if your brand has lots of consumers asking questions, you may want to create FAQ pages on your website and direct your consumers to those pages. Answering everything completely via Twitter may not always be possible, especially when you're restricted to 280 characters per tweet!

Keep in mind that when your customers talk about your brand, they may not always expect or demand a response from you. Knowing when to join Twitter conversations about your brand and, more importantly, how to do so is very much an art. Don't try to join every conversation, and at the same time, don't ignore all conversations. Try to understand the people behind the conversations, think about whether you can add value to it, and then choose to join or not.

4.3.3 Following and followers

The core of activity on Twitter is following other people and getting followed yourself. First and foremost, make sure that you consider following anyone who follows you. Second, consider following all the employees at your company who have Twitter accounts. You'll build goodwill with them, and they'll generate followers for you.

Next, identify influential tweeters who have large followings, and set about following and establishing relationships with them. These people are similar to influential bloggers. They could be experts in a specific domain, with large audiences who can encourage people to follow you and who can influence others. In some cases, they may not be experts but rather celebrities of one kind or another. Friend or Follow (https://friendorfollow.com/twitter/most-followers/) has a list of the most popular people on Twitter by follower count. Not surprisingly, many of them are celebrities, starting with Katy Perry and Justin Bieber. Next on the list are President Obama, Rihanna, Taylor Swift, Lady Gaga, Ellen DeGeneres, Cristiano Ronaldo, YouTube, and Justin Timberlake.

Different applications can help you identify these users, but one we like that measures a user's influence is called Twitalyzer (www.twitalyzer.com). You may want to also try WeFollow (www. wefollow.com), which is a popular Twitter directory that helps you find interesting and influential people and brands to follow. When deciding who to follow, think about it like a cocktail party. First, start with the people you know and the people that they know, and then people talking about subjects important to you, and finally random (or influential!) people and those who approach you.

4.3.4 Marketing via Twitter

At this point, you've done the research on how the Twitter community is talking about you, you've gained a significant following, and you've done *just* the right amount of engagement with your followers. The world of Twitter knows who you are (or at least has an inkling), what you do, and why they need to follow you. That means you can start marketing your products in a more targeted way, starting with how you can do that for free before moving on to the paid tactics.

You can use Twitter to market in a number of ways, but there are a few more urgent and critical ways that you should do so. We list those ways here in order of what we think you should prioritize:

1. **Listening to customers**: Twitter is an incredible platform for you to figure out how your clients consider your items, your organization, and the general business that you're in. Try not to pass up on the chance to tune in to your clients talk about your image progressively. Listen genuinely to your client's worries and utilize the platform to react specifically.

2. **Promoting product launches and events**: Getting news around fast is essential in marketing your products, and there's no social media platform that spreads news faster than Twitter does. Because of this, marketers have the ability to use Twitter in an efficient way to share products and market events to profit on the purpose of the sharing of ads. In fact, marketing

efforts can be shared in this manner. For example, certain big-name brands who have celebrity endorsements in new ads can have these celebrities announce its release on their respective Twitter accounts. A recent example would be the Pepsi commercials for the 2019 Super Bowl. One features singer Cardi B, and she didn't waste any time promoting it on her own Twitter.

3. **Making special deals and discounts**: Promos and discounts are often collaborated with the use of Twitter. Clients answers fast to these Twitter offers and usually disseminate the word to their own followers - retweeting makes that so much easier. Some companies have set up special deal accounts through which they tweet about deals. One example of a company setting up a special deals handle for tweeting about deals on a regular basis is @delloutlet. The Dell Outlet twitter handle has approximately 1.17 million Twitter followers.

4. **Customer service**: Companies use Twitter as an alternative customer service option. They listen for customer complaints and respond to those customers via Twitter itself, or at the very least, they begin the response on Twitter before moving to a phone call or an email exchange. Comcast, JetBlue, and Home Depot are all examples of companies that have successfully used Twitter for customer service.

5. **Engaging meaningfully with customers**: Different companies take different approaches to engaging in a meaningful way with their customers via Twitter.

Nike has a separate account, @NikeSupport, that encourages its community to support each other as well as provide customer support. Whole Foods provides healthful recipes. It also asks its customers what they like to read and watch and then recommends new food podcasts and invites the customers to upcoming company or in-store events.

4.3.5 Promoted accounts on Twitter

Twitter has a huge number of items for publicizing that empower and enable advertisers to achieve clients all the more viably by means of their platform. Among the first of these accessible to publicists are Promoted Accounts, which attracts consideration regarding your Twitter account. In the event that you become tied up with a Promoted Account, you will find in the Who to Follow region your Twitter account name shows up at the correct side of the Twitter screen, with "Advanced" subtitled beneath it.

These Promoted Accounts urge other Twitter clients to pursue your record. You can target who you need to see your Promoted Account by means of a couple of things, for example, topography, interests, and profile portrayals. Advanced Accounts are estimated one of two different ways, which you get the opportunity to choose. They are valued either on an impression premise, which implies that you'll pay for the quantity of individuals who see the Promoted Account posting, or by the quantity of individuals who tail you. The last clearly can differ colossally relying upon purchaser intrigue levels.

While having the most noteworthy number of devotees on Twitter is anything but a genuine proportion of accomplishment, it is significant to develop a solid base of supporters. This will enable you to proceed to fabricate and change over others as they associate with you on the platform.

Promoted Accounts have the additional benefit that after people become your followers, they typically stay your followers. This lasting value differs from display advertising, for which a dollar spent on an impression is lost after the ad campaign has run. You get no real long term benefit from that investment.

4.3.6 Making use of promoted tweets

Promoted Tweets let you draw even more attention to just a single tweet. These Promoted Tweets are mainly sold by being associated to a particular search term. You can select to add a layer focusing on advancement all together for the tweets to contact the general population you truly need to reach.

Beneath you will see the distinctive kinds of Promoted Tweets, and what they are best for:

- **Promoted Tweets in a search**: This is best used to target clients who don't yet tail you or a brand on Twitter. When utilizing this item, you can achieve individual clients through a predetermined pursuit term along these lines to the manner in which Google enables you to promote per the inquiries on its site Google look. Remember that a particular sponsor can buy an inquiry term at any irregular time. Advanced Tweets are purchased through a sale display. Regularly amid the long stretches of an evening, you could see multiple brands competing with one another in real time by buying Promoted Tweets and using the identical search term. In this way, they try to outbid each other for the customer's attention. Promoted Tweets are popular because they allow brands to attach themselves most directly to consumer intent. For example, if you search tweets about holidays, airlines know that you'll probably be thinking about flights, too, and that it is valuable for them to advertise using that phrase.

• **Targeting followers**: Promoted tweets can be used to target followers of your brand on Twitter as well. You may wonder why you should use ads to target followers when they're already following you. But the reality is that when you tweet to your followers, your tweet quickly drops below the fold and can be missed by your followers. When you use Promoted Tweets to target followers, the promoted tweet stays at the top of the feed. As a result, it becomes practically impossible for the follower to miss the tweet.

Promoted tweets are valuable when you want to promote something to your followers — the people who are typically your biggest brand advocates. This strategy works well when you have something to share that you believe will spread organically after it's seeded to a small group of brand loyalists.

• **Geotargeting**: Promoted tweets get even more powerful when you geo-target them at the country or even the DMA level (Nielsen-designated market areas). When you target a Promoted Tweet to just the people in specific locations that matter to you, your Promoted Tweet costs get much lower. This matters most for local businesses who care to advertise only in the actual locations where their businesses exist. Geotargeting can be applied as a layer over any kind of Promoted Tweets.

Promoted Tweets are bought on a cost-per-engagement (CPE) basis versus a cost-per-thousand-impressions (CPM) basis. CPE means that you pay only when a user retweets, replies, clicks, or favorites your tweet. You won't pay for the number of users or people who see the tweet but for those who do something about it or click something because of it. Paying for everyone who saw your tweet alone would be paying on a CPM basis. This fee style creates a system where promoted tweets are very cost effective, and are a performance-based form of spending on social media marketing. It is also for many marketers a nice complement to the many different forms of digital marketing.

4.3.7 Using promoted trends

Twitter is a hopeful internet-based platform for different reasons. However, one component that is significant on Twitter is the manner by which "drifting" subjects work. Each minute inconsistently, Twitter dissects the majority of many discussions occurring on its platform and figures out what is prominent or drifting in a specific minute.

The inclining points you will see get highlighted by the client's feed on the left side. They can be separated by topography too, so for instance, you can see just the drifting points in your general vicinity like the United States or notwithstanding inclining subjects that are imperative just to specific urban communities. What is drifting on Twitter goes about as a gauge of how much a thing might be topical in the physical world at some random minute. Drifting themes are unquestionably not to be missed.

Advanced Trends supplement the natural patterns and help brands to assemble mass mindfulness, influence declarations, to promote item dispatches, talk about occasions coming up, and develop their image by the relationship with other social occasions. They work along these lines to drifting points with the exception of Promoted Trends that are characterized by the publicists. A client sees the Promoted Trend on the left half of the screen with the other slanting themes yet with the word Promoted beneath it.

As with Promoted Tweets, clients can click Promoted Trends to see every one of the tweets containing a certain hashtag or pattern terms related with that Promoted Trend.

Tapping the Promoted puts a user to a search results page that possesses a Paid Tweet from the advertiser at the top of it. Other tweets on the search results page will be unfiltered and open.

Promoted Trends are typically most valuable to buy on days when major pop culture events are happening and then best when aligned in some meaningful form around those pop culture events. For example, when the VMAs (Video Music Awards) air on TV, you might want to buy a Promoted Trend about music or, more specifically, about an award-winning artist from the VMAs because a lot of people will be on Twitter talking about the VMAs.

Promoted Trends are extremely popular with marketers, and it is worth buying the Promoted Trend in advance of the actual day that you want it to run. This is essential because only one Promoted Trend can run on Twitter on a given day, marketers buy those terms well in advance of the actual day that they want the ad to run.

4.3.8 Working with sponsored tweets

One other current advertising opportunity that blends into the paid-tactics domain is Sponsored Tweets. In a similar fashion to sponsored posts on Wogs, some Twitter users with very large followings are open to publishing Sponsored Tweets. Sponsored Tweets are done by speaking directly to Twitter users and securing their interest in posting. You discuss the marketing campaign with willing users and they tweet about your campaign in their own language and style to their own audiences.

Typically, Twitter users publish Sponsored Tweets only if they can disclose the fact that they're sponsored, and if the marketing messages are in sync with their own personal brand and the type of information that they like to share with their followers. Sponsored tweeting is an emergent marketing tactic. An example of a company that provides this service is Sponsored Tweets at http://sponsoredtweets.com/.

4.4 Tips and tricks

Twitter is an adaptable platform and advertisers use it in a wide range of approaches to accomplish their showcasing and business targets. Truth be told, the adaptability of Twitter is the thing that has made it such a significant platform for advertisers. Some utilize it principally for to explore clients, some to advance explicit advertising programs, some for an effort to become influencers, and others for client administration.

Despite how you use it, Twitter causes you to assemble a steadfast, submitted base of adherents. You should remember some key tips and traps when utilizing Twitter to drive up your computerized commitment with them:

● *Provide worth to your customers.*

It is anything but difficult to overlook that Twitter wasn't created as a commitment platform for advertisers to use as an interface with their clients. Or maybe, it was created for individuals to interface with one another, realize what their companions are doing, and communicate their own exercises. For brands to take an interest seriously, they should increase the value of the experience; else, they will be overlooked.

● *Keep in mind that different strategies make sense for different marketing needs.*

Remember that your Twitter procedure needs to line up with your general advertising system. On an instance that your business is about client administration, use Twitter for client administration. If it is for providing exclusive access, use Twitter as a distribution engine for promoting how you provide exclusive access. Match the Twitter tactics to the marketing strategy.

- *Prepare to adjust your Twitter approach.*

There's no better way to evolve your Twitter approach than by paying attention to how your customers respond to your participation during social conversations. Learn from them, and adjust your Twitter approach based on what you see working effectively in real time. Are your customers responding to questions posed by you? Do they shy away from talking about your product? Are they more interested in learning about future marketing activities? Use their participation as a guide for how to market on Twitter.

- *Use Twitter advertising to jump-start conversations.*

Nothing beats organic engagement on Twitter. To be able to hear from your customers in real time, participate in conversations with them, and watch them go about their lives through the conversations that they have on the platform is extremely powerful. However, there are times when you need to use the mass reach of paid advertising to jump-start those engagements or draw special attention to what you're doing. Twitter advertising products help that process.

- *Remember that knowing your customers is as important as ever.*

Some marketers make the mistake of believing that simply because this is a 280-character communication format, you don't need to know your customers as well. That's not true. Before you respond to a tweet from a customer, take a minute to understand who that customer is, what else they tweet about, and what matters to them.

- *Listen, listen, and listen.*

It may be a cliché, but it's still very true. Listening to how your customers talk to each other about culture, about your products' category, your products, and your company is critical to succeeding on Twitter. Listening is the first step in participating in conversations — a step that must not be skipped.

On a final note, you can also make use of what is called Twitter Cards. The cards provide a summary of your Twitter business information along with your tweet. They require a bit of html to be added to your website.

Hopefully, you now understand how Twitter could be potentially beneficial in the promotion of your brand and your products.

Chapter 5

Instagram

5.0 Introduction

Whether you are a newbie to Instagram or not, you still stand to learn a lot from this chapter, especially when it comes to applying it to marketing. If you *are* new to the application, though, learning about it here will probably convince you to finally give it a try. It has, after all, made big waves since its release in 2010 and it's a feat that you've been able to stay off it for this long!

In July 2012, Instagram's growth blew up even more when it was acquired by Facebook. Similar to Pinterest and Tumblr, Instagram is a platform that allows its users to share visual content with incredible ease. It also kind of serves as a photo editor since you have a range of photo filters to choose from when editing before posting. The main difference between Instagram and Tumblr or Pinterest is that Instagram focuses on users' and marketers' original content whereas the other two are primarily images that are already online and shared amongst the community.

In this chapter, we'll go over the basics of Instagram before moving on to how both personal users and marketers can use it to build a relationship with the community. You'll learn more about editing photos, developing a storyline, discovering others, and getting yourself discovered.

5.1 Instagram for The Uninitiated

Instagram is primarily a mobile application, though it is also viewable on computers. However, it's better utilized on mobile, as it's much easier to snap photos and post them immediately from there. The first step, then, is to download the application for your iOS, Android, or Windows gadgets.

That is, you should download the application when you're sure that you can reach your target demographic using this platform. To help you determine that a little easier, let's take a look at the 2019 statistics projection reported by Hootsuite:

Instagram has 1 billion users, 50% of whom use the platform every day.

80% of users are located outside the U.S.

60% of users have discovered products on Instagram.

72% of users have bought a product they've seen on Instagram.

In its report called "Social Media 2013 Update," Pew Research says that:

Twenty percent of female U.S. adults and 15 percent of male adults use Instagram.

The largest user age group is 18-29.

If this sounds like the audience that you want to reach, you need to jump on the platform right away! Join the 25% of the Fortune 500 companies that also consider Instagram vital in their own marketing campaigns.

According to a study by L2-Intelligence, about 93% of luxury brands like Cartier, Chanel, Dior, Calvin Klein, and Versace are on Instagram. If you take a quick look at their profiles, you'll see that they are able to produce high quality visual content that looks great on their profile page. As a company, that's exactly what you're aiming for too!

5.1.1 Signing up

So after you've downloaded the application onto your device, you need to set up your account. Register with your email or Facebook account, though we personally suggest the former so it's more professional. It's as easy as that! You can choose to make your account public or private, but for purpose of this chapter, we're using the model of a public Instagram account (since you don't want a company account that's private).

5.1.2 Exploring the app

Take a look at the bottom of your screen when you open up the application. You'll see a few icons that'll take you to different places in the app. Here's a brief rundown of what these icons mean:

- **Home**: This is where you see all photos posted by the people you follow.

- **Explore**: Here you can search for topics of interest or see what the app recommends for you based on who you follow.

- **Camera**: What you click when you want to take a photo directly from the app. You can either take a new one, or choose from those already in your device's photo library.

- **Following**: This is where you see your followers' activity - who recently followed you, liked or commented on your posts, or new posts in hashtags you recently viewed.

- **Your photos**: Photos you have taken and uploaded to instagram.

5.1.3 Using filters

As we mentioned earlier, Instagram has its own filters that you can use to edit your photos. Of course, you can also leave your photos as it is, that's entirely up to you. In fact, it was reported that 50% of users do not use any of the filters.

The filters give the photos a specific effect, like making it brighter or darker, enhancing the warm and cool undertones, or rendering it completely black and white. The top five filters used on Instagram as of this writing are Normal, EarlyBird, X-Pro II, Valencia, and Rise. You may also opt to use other photo-taking or editing apps to get the effect you desire before posting them onto Instagram.

Other advanced in-app parameters which will help you enhance or upgrade your filters are as follows:

- **Filters**: The filters now have a slider that allows you to see how much of the effect you want to apply.

- **Vignette**: In addition to the Tilt-Shift tool, you can now use the Vignette tool to create a blurry black border around the photo.

- **Cropping and straightening**: You can use these photos to cut your photos to your desired size, or maybe even tilt it a little off-center.

5.1.4 Getting Found on Instagram

You're all set up now and can navigate your way around the app. So what's next, you ask? What's next is that you want to be discovered.

Who doesn't love a good hashtag? What started on Twitter has migrated to Instagram, and it really helps you get found. On Instagram though, some people can really get carried away with their hashtags. Every social media platform has its own unspoken guidelines for hashtags - obviously on Twitter it's limited because of the character count, and Facebook doesn't really *have* a hashtag culture. However, Instagram embraces hashtags, so you can use them to your heart's content. Just remember that as a business, you should choose your hashtags wisely.

Hashtags are vital in a marketing campaign as they will help you really expand your reach, even to those who aren't already in your community of followers. It will also make it easier for you to track how people are engaging with your brand, especially if you have hashtags customized for your company.

For these reasons, it is prudent for you to look at what hashtags are currently being used and what new ones you should create. One way to find out this information is to look at search tools for hashtags. Some of these hashtag tools include:

1. **Talkwalker** (http://talkwalker.com): Free/Fee versions. This tool has lots of value. You can see the

performance of a hashtag and much more; for example, you can see the influencers who use it and whether the sentiment about it is positive or negative.

2. **RiteTag** (http://ritetag.com): Free! One of the great features of this tool is that it will go over the hashtags you have used in Twitter and tell you whether they are overused or unlikely to be seen. Obviously, you won't use this tool for a new Instagram campaign.

3. **Tagboard** (https://tagboard.com): Free/Fee versions. What's so useful about this tool is that you can build tagboards that display specific hashtags, making it easy to see what's happening.

Check these out to see how helpful it can be to analyze and evaluate your hashtags.

5.1.5 Structuring Instagram for Business Goals

As you can see, Instagram is a social media giant that has enormous potential for almost every business. An obvious clue to its value is that it was purchased by and is highly integrated with Facebook. Many small and medium-sized marketers have yet to take advantage of it, though. One reason is that they are already overwhelmed by the number of social media platforms that they feel required to use.

Don't be one of these marketers. Look carefully at which platforms you choose to devote your time and budget to. If a platform is large but not right for your user base, don't get pulled into using it because everyone uses it. If you feel that you can build relevant and engaging visual content for your brand, then Instagram is a great place to set up a social media marketing campaign.

5.1.6 Creating Content For Your Business

As with any social platform you choose, you want to develop relationships with a community of like-minded people who can become your customers. On Instagram, images serve as the main tool and the stories they tell.

To help your team focus on uploading the right images for the company, it's helpful to create a list of category stories to which your staff can refer. You want your staff to easily generate new photos and videos and not miss the great moments to capture.

For example, some story categories could be the following:

- **Working in the community**: pictures of charity events and training sessions with users.

- **Community member photos**: encourage users to send in photos depicting their use of the product.

- **Our pets at work**: Adorable pet photos that humanize your staff and make connections with other pet lovers who can upload their photos.

- **Contests**: Photos of contest entries by users and winner photos.

- **Featured staff members**: Video of staff members giving a video greeting (fifteen seconds long at most).

● **Request for product improvements**: Photos of current products with questions from the company about how to improve them. Customers are asked to reply to these questions and offer some ideas of their own.

● **Inspiring photos just because**: A beautiful image from nature or daily life to make others feel good.

Engaging users by using consistent story themes is the best approach. When users see a new image, they can relate it to all the other images that have made up that storyline for your brand. This creates a "series" feeling that keeps visitors coming back for more. Think of it like a TV show with particular stories that are continually updated.

Here are two other items that your staff should pay attention to:

1. **Hashtags**: As discussed earlier, hashtags are how people find your content. Make sure to use ones that are already in use that relate to your brand. Using them is a habit people already have. In addition, create specific hashtags for your brand.

2. **Captions**: Every photo should have a caption. We are trained to look for them and read them. Therefore, captions are an important part of the marketing process on Instagram. Don't assume that they are optional. Users have been shown to favor long ones, so give careful thought to what you write. Be creative!

5.1.7 Curating and Sharing

Key to everything you do on Instagram is the idea that sharing will create buzz and new followers. Hand-in-hand with content creation is the manner in which you share it to your audience. As we said, you are presenting stories. The best way to do that pretty much speaks for itself on Instagram - by using the platform's Stories feature.

5.2 Instagram stories

In August 2016, Instagram launched what is probably their most successful feature to date - Instagram Stories. In today's fast-paced world, not everyone has time to spend hours and hours browsing through apps like Instagram - no matter how beautiful all the photos are. With the Stories feature, brands now have around 10 to 15 seconds to basically pitch whatever they're advertising - themselves, their products, or what-have-you. Your Stories are posted immediately to the Homepage of everyone who follows you.

As a marketer, there are many ways that you can take advantage of this. Because you can post photos *and* videos, there's really no limit to the content that you can create. You can post a plain background with bold text that advertises your next contest or a clickable link to your website; you can post short videos showing a glimpse of how your products are made - the possibilities are endless!

In 2018, Instagram added even more features to Stories that allow you to make more dynamic, interactive posts. Some of these include:

- **Clickable links**: Viewers can be redirected immediately to your blog, website, or even another account when they click on the links.

- **Polls**: You can put an interactive poll on your Stories to immediately engage your customers and gain insight. For example, you could ask about opinions on color combinations on products, or what dish they'd like to see cooked up next. Your poll could be about anything curated to your brand.

- **Quick reactions**: Viewers can now react to your video immediately, without having to leave a comment or direct message. This is useful to marketers in order to discover whether users love or hate that specific advertisement.

- **Auto video segmentation**: When the feature first launched, users needed to rush to fit everything into the 15-second limit. Now, you can post longer videos and the app will automatically split it up into 15-second increments for you - it's seamless and effortless, and you don't need to rush through any dialogue or text to force it to fit.

- **Share to Stories**: This is very useful in customer engagement. You're now able to share other people's content to your Stories, where it will link back to the original content. So, if you're doing cross-promotional content with other users or brands, this is great! Or if a customer posts an A++ amazing review about your brand, you can share it to your Stories so that your other followers can see how amazing you are. Think of it as similar to retweeting.

One potentially problematic aspect of Instagram Stories when it was introduced was that it would only appear on your followers' Homepage for 24 hours before it's archived.

However, this problem was solved in December 2017 with Instagram Highlights.

5.2.1 Instagram highlights

In order for Instagram stories not to disappear after a day, Instagram introduced the Highlights feature. Users are now able to save their stories to specifically curated galleries on their profiles.

So taking from the examples in the previous section for story categories, a company could have one Highlight focused on "Community Work", another for "Featured Employee", and yet another for "Contests". There's no limit to the number of Highlights you can create, but you can only have 100 Stories per Highlight.

By making use of the Highlights feature, your followers can keep coming back to your Stories if they need information after 24 hours of it being posted.

5.2.2 IGTV

Instagram TV was also introduced in mid-2018, but it has yet to really take off. IGTV is the YouTube of Instagram and allows you to post long-form content that is specifically produced for the platform. It's not like Facebook Live or Instagram Stories which allows you to stream in real time.

So if you feel that 15 seconds of segmented content on Instagram Stories just doesn't cut it, you might want to consider building a profile on IGTV. Though it is built directly into the Instagram app for viewers, you'll have to download the IGTV app to create and upload content.

If you are creating and displaying only your own pictures and not finding and sharing other people's content, you are talking to, essentially, yourself. You also need to spread other people's stories to demonstrate that you are interested in more than just your own company's activities. If your brand has a strong visual campaign, Instagram is the perfect place for your marketing strategies.

Some brands known for their success on Instagram include Oreo, Nike, Gucci, and WeWork. Check out their profiles if you want an idea for how to build your own Instagram presence!

Chapter 6

YouTube

6.0 Introduction

YouTube is another social platform that has had explosive growth since its launch in 2005. It is now the number one website for online videos and whenever marketers think of viral marketing, they often think in terms of YouTube. You can't afford to overlook it as a marketing vehicle, due to its importance to consumers and its potential reach.

In this chapter, we will discuss briefly about YouTube basics before moving to how you as a marketer can create customized content for your subscribers. We give some tips on how you can interact with your viewers and finally, how you can seed a viral campaign.

6.1 YouTube In One Glance

If you think that YouTube is not a large force in the marketing space, consider the following facts:

If YouTube were a cable network, it would be the largest one.

Approximately 80 percent of the traffic on YouTube is from outside the United States.

YouTube accounts for 28 percent of all Google searches and is the world's second largest search engine after Google.

Mobile views already represent 25 percent of all YouTube video views globally.

Clearly, YouTube has all the muscle you need to drive your *video* social media marketing efforts. You can't afford not to utilize it.

6.2 Why Social Media Marketing on YouTube?

The principal thing you have to ask yourself is the amount of cash you prefer to spend on placing ads on YouTube. You realize that you need to take part, yet you aren't sure how much time or exertion to dedicate to it. To enable you to choose, here are a few advantages you can get from showcasing on YouTube:

- **Visibility**: Most importantly, being on YouTube puts you directly amidst where the activity is. Individuals come to YouTube to search for recordings, and you need your video pieces to be found.

- **Branding**: Stretching out your marking to the recordings you make is really direct. Your logo and other structure things ought to dependably be available, which causes you with brand acknowledgment. On the off chance that you don't have these components, you will need to get them for every social medium advertising endeavors.

- **Fees are not required when setting up**: As opposed to setting up a site, transferring a video on YouTube and making a channel is free. On an instance that you as of now have recordings you've made, everything to do is join. See the area later where we talk about how to "Alter Your YouTube

Content". You must also be aware of your expenses like the maintenance of your videos.

● **Fixed placement selections**: You should not be stressed over how your video will look or be set and output on the site. Yours will be shown close by the various recordings. Your objective at that point ought to clearly be the means by which to emerge, not how to fit in. In the event that you have a designer who can utilize the YouTube API to enable you to emerge, then you are in a colossal favorable position.

● **Optimized already for search engines**: Because of the inherent website improvement organization of the webpage, Google shows your recordings in its query items. In any case, you should give careful consideration to the catchphrases that are utilized to portray recordings with the goal that they get the extra consideration they merit.

6.3 Getting People to Subscribe to Your Channel

Individuals on YouTube who patronize your channel are known as your endorsers. Each time you transfer another video, they get advised, and their names and symbols have appeared to you on your YouTube channel page.

Think about the supporters as your devotees on Twitter and adherents on Instagram or even fans on Facebook pages. Similarly, as you would support those connections on those other social platforms, you ought to do likewise here as well. You will ask, what's the most ideal approach to assemble a bunch of subscribers on Youtube? Consider doing the following:

1. **Quality is better than quantity**.

You've presumably heard that when you are on the web, "quality written substance makes all the difference." Think about your substance for your YouTube channel as you would for a TV channel. On the off chance that the substance is feeble, you won't manufacture a network of endorsers who clatter for additional. It is not required though to have a Hollywood level quality, however you do need to extend a particular polished methodology and consistency.

1. **Great strategies provide better results**

Don't simply consider you are direct as far as one video at any given moment yet rather as a channel where you'll distribute explicit bits of substance all through occasions of the year — some will be instructive, some more for diversion, and some news-centered recordings that offer some incentive to your watchers and construct your image in the meantime.

1. Promote video commenting

Remarks on YouTube are much the same as the remarks you'd see on online journals or other internet based life like Facebook. Some have esteem; some are simply senseless or jabber. You will likely make a network of individuals who acknowledge and anticipate your transferred recordings. In case they post remarks that demonstrate that you are satisfying them, you've met your objective.

1. Subscribe to other people's videos

There are two qualities in buying in to other individuals' recordings. The first is you get the opportunity to perceive what the experience resembles. You need to see how it feels to buy in and what different ways channel proprietors draw in with their endorsers so you can impersonate this for your very own supporters. Furthermore, it allows you to meet and impart to others on their page. They are keen on getting supporters just as you are as well. Keep in mind, this page is a social platform.

1. Utilize your videos by sharing it on other platforms

The main reason why you need to do this is that you will build and get more supporters. It likewise enhances your picture on those different platforms. In any case, as you begin to share your clasps somewhere else, dependably put the video on YouTube first and insert from YouTube as opposed to transferring straightforwardly to the site you're sharing on. The only exemption might be Facebook, where you can transfer specifically and perhaps you'll have higher commission rates with your video by transferring the video straightforwardly to Facebook.

6.4 Promoting on YouTube

Realizing how to distribute and advance your video reach is vital to getting them the consideration they merit. Coming up next are a few suggestions you can follow while advancing your video cuts on YouTube.

Having a committed YouTube channel for your organization or brand is imperative since it enables you to feature all related video cuts in a single spot. A YouTube channel will go about as your image's record home, and where cuts that you have distributed can show up. Setting up a channel is exceptionally simple, so don't hesitate to do such.

A channel likewise gives you a chance to make a profile for yourself and have a spot to interface your site. Make a point to alter the channel to coordinate your organization or your image's visual character. You don't have to physically make your YouTube channel. When you agree to accept a record, utilize the "Make Account" connect in the upper right corner of the landing page, and transfer a video cut. A channel will be naturally made for you. To achieve your YouTube channel, simply click your username after you sign in. It's as simple as that!

In addition, remember to give a connection to and from your site to your YouTube channel. Additionally, ensure that your different channels, similar to your Facebook page and online journals, likewise have connections to your YouTube channel. Complementary connections are critical to a reasonable and brief internet based life showcasing effort.

6.5 Modify your YouTube content

Putting up TV ads on the platform is not enough itself because it will be subpar if you do not modify it according to the style of the format of the platform for it to become effective. It is crucial to optimize the ads to the preference of the viewers at all times.

You must also attempt to limit the time of your videos, preferably fewer than 5 minutes, so that the size of the file will not be too high. In fact, the usual length of a footage is about a little more than 4 minutes. You must also categorize your videos into themed playlist so that it will be much easier to access by people.

For various instances, a quick footage that lasts just a few minutes can have a huge effect. You are trying to get your audience to disseminate your video in the various platforms. This being said, you can't anticipate the viewers to exert a lot of effort on a single video. The fact that the site has a massive number of users and content is enough to explain why it will be a challenge for your content to be seen.

Developers at YouTube seem to have a learned a thing or two from the success of Instagram stories, because they've introduced the exact same feature on YouTube. Creators can now post short Stories that are displayed to their subscribers. As a marketer, you can use these Stories to tease content that's lined up for future release.

6.6 Tag and categorize everything you upload

Like the other social media platforms discussed, YouTube has also introduced the concept of tagging and categorizing its content. Make sure that you choose the best and most appropriate tags and categories for your content! The last thing you want is to be reaching out to the wrong consumers who have no interest or need for your products. Start by looking for videos in your industry and see what tags they're using.

Of course, your content may not be an exact fit in one category but you can resolve this by seeing which category has the most videos similar to yours. Then you can use customized tags to fill up the holes left by the limits in categorization. YouTube lets you add an unlimited number of tags, so your options are literally limitless. These tags, like hashtags, make it easier for users to find your content if they're viewing something similar.

Use YouTube's email and bulletins, too, if that fits in with your company's marketing goals. This will help with the promotion of your clips as email subscribers will receive regular updates about your content or will even recommend you to those viewing similar content as yours. The bulletins and stories feature also allows you to update your current subscribers.

Just be careful that you're not being too spammy, as this'll turn off a lot of subscribers and users. If they haven't asked for an email, don't email them.

6.7 Make response videos

A common way that YouTube content creators interact and expand their reach is by collaborating with each other. One way to do this is to make response videos! You can make use of this strategy with other videos that are in your niche. However, remember to keep it civil and respectful - you're NOT going to do yourself any good if you are judgmental.

Procter and Gamble utilized this system to make impact on its prevalent Old Spice fellow campaign with Isaiah Mustafa. In the first place, the organization made an entertaining video advancing the item. At that point, it followed up by making video reactions by Mustafa to the remarks made on the web. This rose on the ubiquity of the first video and made the watchers return for an additional one. The incredible news about this system is that despite the fact that it's modest, it can pack a punch. Envision the shock of your watchers when you react to their remarks with a video customized for them.

6.8 Include a call to action

Every good commercial on TV should leave you with the feeling that you should go out and buy or do what they told you to do. That particular tactic is called a "call to action". Your YouTube content should be no different - just lose the hard sell and don't be so glaringly obvious about it. Always link back to your site, or slip in a short skit about buying merchandise. You could even include contact details for your viewers to reach out to if they want to learn more or engage in more conversation. This is an opportunity to generate sale, so don't forget your calls to action!

Additionally, unlike TV commercials, there's no need to wait until the end before you include the call to action in your YouTube video. The link can be suspended on a part of the video throughout the whole thing, or you can slip it in halfway - it's all up to you!

6.9 Important Note: Have fun, too!

YouTube is entertainment central - its users flock to the platform seeking videos to entertain them. That means that you, as a creator, should be giving them something entertaining too! Even if the nature of your content is educational or informational, there's never anything wrong with injecting a little bit of humor every now and then. Take a look at the channel Crash Course, which covers all things educational, or BuzzFeed Unsolved's "Ruining History" videos - they're very informational, but it's definitely not a classroom lecture!

When producing your videos, ask yourself if it's something that you would watch - that's always the best way to go. Also remember that the first few seconds are the most crucial in capturing and keeping your audience's attention. Start off energized and try to sustain that, otherwise you'll lose your viewers as your video goes on.

6.10 Creating a Viral Campaign

Viral recordings are of two kinds, and it is vital to be comfortable with them:

1. Organic: This is the kind of video that makes a universal furor, and heaps of individuals hurry to see it and offer it with their companions (for instance: Psy's Korean melody Gangnam Style, which is perhaps the most seen video ever all around, with in excess of 2 billion perspectives). Ordinarily, it simply happens naturally absent much by way of arranging. It catches the creative ability of watchers and goes and detonates.

2. Seeded: This kind of video has a cautiously arranged crusade for turning into a web sensation with especially thought behind it and publicizing dollars to spend. It may circulate around the web, however, there is no surety. A few organizations have practical experience in influencing recordings to have viral seeding, or you can even go to general web-based social networking offices to get help. Organizations like Sharethrough (www.sharethrough.com), TubeMogul (www.tubemogul.com), and Tubular (www.tubularlabs.com) can help in such manner.

Would you be able to influence a video to turn into a web sensation? Determinedly not. If you can, advertisers would dispatch them by the armload. In any case, these few hints and traps may enhance your odds of making a viral video.

1. Keep the substance new: Nothing beats new substance with regards to making viral video cuts. The substance should be so captivating and extraordinary that individuals can't resist

the urge to need to impart it to everybody they know. Continuously begin by concentrating on the substance.

2. Use big names if conceivable: In case you are speaking to a major brand and can utilize big names, use them. Don't speculate about doing that, do it. Adding superstars to the storyline commonly makes the recordings turn out to be progressively popular. We're a big name fixated advanced culture, and VIPs drive sees particularly in popular culture today. It is as fundamental as that. The absolute most mainstream publicizing recordings amid the World Cup, Super Bowl, and other huge brandishing occasions every single utilized VIP.

3. Make it strange: A video that you need to watch a few times over and offer to your companions is typically a video that has a dreamlike component in it. Somebody is accomplishing something in the video that is exceptionally strange or extremely insane and you can't help watch it rehashed occasions or converse with others about it. Better also is if a big name or acclaimed individual is accomplishing something dreamlike.

4. Implore feelings: Brain science has demonstrated that the recordings that draw in the most consideration and are shared most frequently are the ones that entreat feelings in the watcher. This happens regardless of whether those feelings are of wonder, of indignation, about diversion, or about sicken. Albeit some of the time dreamlike recordings are regularly the ones that get shared frequently, don't overlook alternate ways which you could stimulate the feelings of any potential watcher. Also, remember that recordings that beg a scope of

feelings are normally the ones that play out the most ideal way since they are progressively multidimensional.

5. Make it short: Individuals online normally don't have much time. You should keep the viral little clasp short. Some of the time cuts as short as ten seconds are sufficiently long for a video to possibly turn into a web sensation. Likewise make sure to concentrate on quality rather than quantity. In addition, recall that there aren't any rigid tenets for what the recommended length of a YouTube video ought to be.

6. Don't make it an advertisement: Commonly, advertisers cannot avoid the impulse to transform pretty much anything into commercial. The substance should be seen and experienced as stimulation. The ideal method to engage an objective client is to consider taking a gander at everything else they are likely review on YouTube and after that utilization those as a benchmark to appreciate what style of substance they would be most inspired by.

You would likewise complete a viral seeding effort on a financial plan. Someone inside your association could be responsible for making a crusade that would be produced. You should pick how high the stakes are and what the general objective is.

Viral seeding is the ability to disseminate footages in a specific niche to improve its share-ability. That can mean including the following:

- **Targeting influencers**: If you have a lot of connections on a certain niche, then you can advertise the content of the videos.

- **Advertising**: Video proprietors purchase various kinds of advertising — Google, YouTube, Facebook, etc. — to elevate the chances of sharing.

- **Creating resonance**: Integrating the videos in a more profound and truthful that everyone can incorporate themselves to will increase the probability of your videos trending.

- **Placing it on social networks**: Connects the footage to Facebook posts, tweets etc.

- **Partnerships**: Partnering with popular YouTubers to aide in promoting the videos can create a lot of improvement.

- **Emailing it to popular lists**: Famous newsletters have the privilege to put a link to the footage.

- **Blogging**: Popular bloggers integrate a link to the footage in some of their posts.

- **Putting up giveaways**: Giving freebies can increase the number of viewers for the footage.

An instance of viral seeding happening is a campaign Unilever made for one of its brands in 2013; Dove. It was in April of that year, Unilever propelled a YouTube video wherein a few ladies portray themselves to a measurable sketch craftsmen. In the meantime the craftsmen who are doing the outlining can't see their subject. Later in the video, similar ladies are depicted by outsiders whom they had met the earlier day. In only one single week, the video had accomplished in excess of 15 million perspectives from around the world. An article about the video was shared on Mashable multiple times within 24 hours. One primary motivation behind why the video performed so well was it depended on an amazing all-inclusive human truth which is something that each lady could identify with and get it. The substance was new, sincerely established, and did not feel like a promotion for the Dove magnificence item by any means.

In case you're an advertiser of a huge brand, you may have the dollars to put resources into some paid publicizing strategies. YouTube gives a few alternatives depending on your destinations. They arrange the destinations as Brand Awareness, Product Launch, Direct Response, and Reputation Management.

After you've decided your goal, you are offered advertisement positions including the following:

• Home-page promotions: This furnishes the sponsor with a debut spot on the YouTube landing page. In excess of 50 million exceptional clients go there consistently. It's prime promoting land.

• TrueView Videos advertisements: YouTube presented this promotion design a couple of years back that enables clients to click a Skip This Ad Now catch after the client has seen the promotion for five seconds. With this prominent organization, promoters are roused to make the initial five seconds of their recordings especially fascinating.

• Brand channel: This classification offers a few dimensions of customization for a channel committed to your image. The customizations incorporate how the page looks, what recordings are advanced and how clients are attracted to it. This is unique in relation to a client channel, which is free when you join.

● Mobile: Video promotions are served up on your client's cell phones iPhone, Android, and BlackBerry. Score records YouTube as the main goal for portable video.

With these paid strategies, YouTube furnishes all the standard media measurements with YouTube Insights. These incorporate impressions, snap to play, active clicking factor, and quartile saw notwithstanding the network measurements (likes, perspectives, and remarks). A quartile see demonstrates the information portioned in equivalent quarters with the goal that you can decide how well each is getting along. Additionally incorporated into the measurements are socioeconomics, areas of viewership, watcher sources (where the clients originated from to see the video), and the amount of the video they saw. These measurements are illuminating to the point that they are presently constraining promoters to reevaluate how they make recordings.

Llikewise, you can focus on these notices to keep running while you also select an accomplice content. This situation matters to numerous advertisers who stress over what their very own promotions (video or something else) may show up beside.

At the conclusion of this module, you should now have an improved grasp of how you can put your video marketing campaigns - if there are some - onto the YouTube platform. It takes a while to build up a significant following but if you do it right, you'll be a YouTube sensation before you know it.

Chapter 7

Pinterest

7.0 Introduction

Imagine that someone came to the virtual lobby of your business (or your real lobby) and offered to create a fabulous wall of your brand images and products. It would be colorful and contain clear labeling. The most exciting thing about this wall is that if you point at one of the images, you're taken to a screen that tells you more about the product and helps you buy it. That's an offer you wouldn't turn down. Well, that's what Pinterest offers your business — and it's free!

In March 2010, Pinterest launched its beta. It was met with polite applause from friends and colleagues of the startup. But not many people were understand how to use it. At the later year, it was listed in Time Magazine's 50 Best Websites of 2011. Omnicore Agency stated that as of September 2018, Pinterest has 250 million active users monthly, 50% of whom are outside of the United States. It now has over 3 billion boards and more than 175 billion pins.

For the uninitiated, a "pin" is anything and everything that a user uploads to their profiles - photos, videos, recipes, what-have-you. It's the *individual*, stand-alone content. Other users can then share this pin to their own profiles - what's also called "pinning". On the other hand, a board is a category - all similar pins can be lumped together in a board.

So going back - what caused this explosion of interest? The answer is visuals! It provided a fool-proof way for people to share pictures of things they liked and perhaps wanted to buy. Because of the ease with which users can post external links on their photos, it was just a quick hop from pinning pictures to a digital board to buying them online. According to the Social Intelligence Report Q4 2013 Adobe Digital Index, Pinterest's revenue per visit is up 244 percent year over year and 69 percent quarter over quarter. That's pretty an amazing growth!

To optimize your use of Pinterest as a business tool, you need to understand how members use it. If you are already a user, you're ahead of the game. If you have never used it, help yourself by exploring it first as a user would.

In this chapter, we look at how to get started with Pinterest, find interesting pins, collaborate with colleagues, distribute marketing materials, and sell products. You'll also have some fun along the way!

7.1 Recognizing Pinterest Users

As you know, visuals instantly attract your eye. Your brain understands them more quickly than the written word and is more likely to respond to them. Posts with images have a greater response on all the social networks.

To understand the attraction of Pinterest, you need look no further than the home page. It contains hundreds of images of things you personally like and respond to. How does it do this? Take a look at getting started with Pinterest and you'll see how social media marketing with Pinterest can attract new customers.

As a baseline, it's important to note that Pinterest users are approximately 70 percent female (majority of users between the ages of 25 and 44) and 30 percent male. If women are not your target audience, however, don't turn away just yet. You have several important reasons to consider Pinterest as a social media marketing tool:

1. **Large number of users**: As we said, Pinterest is growing every day. You have an active group of women (50 percent of whom have children) who are happy to re-pin. They wish to recommend items as well as buy for family members. We've also seen reports that men are starting to catch up and use Pinterest for organizing information like travel info and hobbies.
2. **Good distribution tool**: Sharing is the order of the day. You never know who will share something on your website. One person could pin your photo, and

their connections will pin it from there, and the sharing train just continues!

3. **Easy sales tools**. Selling from the gift section is very easy; you just have to put a link to your store to redirect Pinterest users to the products on your website.

4. **Excellent showcase:** Based on the way the system is constructed clearly and and clean-cut way, almost every pin looks good. Why not take advantage of that?

5. **A lot of time spent pinning**. Because a user's homepage *only* has photos that they're interested in, they typically spend more than 15 minutes looking around. That's a long time to hold consumer attention.

Over the next few pages, we focus on Pinterest for business. If you want to familiarize yourself before signing up as a business, you can sign up with a personal account. It's easy to convert to a business account - it's literally just a click of a button!

7.2 Exploring the Interests of Users

To see topics of interest to you, Pinterest suggests that you choose five boards to start. When you begin, the site displays a text link at the top of your page that says, "Want to see more Pins you love in your feed? Follow interesting boards." Click that link and choose your topics.

Users have lots of other ways to find interesting pins. You may just type keywords into the search box and see what comes up. Another alternative is to click the button next to the search box with the lines on it (signifying a list). When you click this button, a window pops up, displaying all the categories you can choose your interests from.

One way to see what's hot on pinterest is to check out its "popular" board by clicking that category link. Going to this link shows you what people are currently pinning and may give you some ideas.

7.3 Pinning As A Social Activity

Pinterest makes finding and sharing pins a truly social activity. Previously it would have been a marketer's dream to have potential customers trading pictures of their products and commenting on them. Now, customers can go right to the source of the pin and buy the product.

Features like re-pinning, liking, and commenting create targeted groups with common interests who can also recommend your product to friends.

In the interconnectedness of social media platforms, it's important to make it easy for users to pin from whatever platform they're on. Download the following for your pinterest site to help your users out:

- **A pin widget for your website**: Having a website pin lets users pin anything on your site to their Pinterest account.

- **A board widget**: This widget lets you embed your favorite Pinterest board (displaying up to 30 pins) on your website so that visitors can see a representative sample. Your goal is to entice people who visit your website to go to your Pinterest account

7.3.1 Focusing on Strategy

Now that you've seen Pinterest through the eyes of a user, this section tells you about three key ways to use Pinterest to achieve your business goals:

1. **Use the power of visuals to attract followers.**

First and foremost, you need to think of Pinterest as a gigantic billboard for your company that can be seen by millions. Users can find images in all sorts of ways because they are pinned and re-pinned. You never know how many people you can reach until you start pinning and getting feedback. You can see what's popular and determine how to create more content of that type.

1. **Develop cross promotion.**

Cross promotion to and from Pinterest will power up your other marketing efforts and is the key to optimizing your use of Pinterest. Every one of your social media channels should provide the capability for users to pin items to Pinterest and then send them to other channels. For example, a user can pin from your website to Pinterest, and on Pinterest you can provide a link to your blog.

Or, say that you're planning a new marketing campaign that includes all sorts of exciting graphics and new pages. Make sure that all those items get pinned to a board that supports the campaign with the same discounts and promotions. With this strategy, you leverage what you've already created.

1. **Leverage your existing business strategy.**

Although leveraging your current business strategy might seem obvious, it is often overlooked. Because Pinterest is so different from other social networks, businesses hold it apart from their other business strategies. Actually, it is the perfect complement to any marketing plan. The key is to determine how it serves your current interests. As you develop a strategy for using Pinterest, remember to create hashtags that support your goals. Users can also use the hashtags they want, but don't leave it to chance if you have some strategic goals. For example, if you are planning a major conference and have developed hashtags, be sure to use them on your pins.

7.4 Becoming a Business Pinner

To get started with Pinterest for Business, go to http://business.pinterest.com/en and enter your email address or your Facebook login. Getting started is easy and free! After you have signed up and chosen your name, you can start creating boards of topics that interest you, and pin items to them.

Don't forget that if you want to pin to any of your boards from your mobile device, you need to download the iPhone app in the iTunes store or the Android app from Google Play.

7.4.1 Setting up your profile

In this section, you can explore how you might set your profile as business user. As a business user, you want to make your brand clear and understandable. This section looks at how two lifestyle companies list themselves on Pinterest. One uses a person as a brand, Martha Stewart, Inc.; the other, L.L.Bean, uses the company brand. Both do a great job of conveying what their brands have to offer, but they do it in different ways. By looking at each type, you can see what might work for you.

You don't have to be a giant conglomerate to succeed. Millions of people are enjoying and buying from small and midsize businesses, too.

When you sign up as a business, the profile sections for Pinterest boards are Name, Picture, Username, About You, Location, and Website. Here's what Martha Stewart and L.L. Bean do to communicate with customers.

7.4.2 Example profile: Martha Stewart (MS)

Martha Stewart, who is known for her beautiful presentations of food, crafts and home design, uses Pinterest to its full visual advantage. Her main website is http://www.marthastewart.com/.

- **Name**: In this case, the name "Martha Stewart Living" is used. She names her boards in a way that helps her bridge the gap between personal and business. Give some careful thought to the name you want to use to identify your company. If you are a "solopreneur" or small business owner you can use your name and, in the description, list the name of your business. It depends on how closely you are identified with your brand.

- **Picture**: The name you chose previously would dictate the picture you use for your profile. If your name and face are part of the brand, you use your own picture. If you're not, you use your logo. Even though some companies have a logo, they use their CEO's picture because that person has "celebrity" status. For Martha Stewart, you see her own picture.

- **Username**: This is the URL by which your site will be identified. For example, MS has https://www.pinterest.com/marthastewart/.

- **About You**: This descriptive content shows up beneath your name and serves as a description of you and your brand. Here's where MS incorporates both her personal boards and her company boards in the same place, for a total of a whopping 165 boards. Along with her boards Around, My Farm and My Pets, you also can connect to her departments for Living, Weddings, Crafts, and Products. The links take you to instructional information that has value for the reader. The site has no hard sell and the text comes across in an authentic manner. The company focus is to be the authority on how to create a beautiful life so she mixes crafts with recipes, gardening and everything in between.

- **Location**: MS lists New York, NY, as where her business is located. Previously, it was listed as Kaitolah, where she actually has a home, not a business. You can opt to use either of these options for your own location.

- **Website**: MS links to her website (you must have your site verified by Pinterest). You can also link to Twitter and Facebook.

7.4.3 Example profile: LL Bean

The main page on Pinterest for L.L. Bean displays the following:

- **Name**: The company name used is L.L. Bean.

- **Picture**: The company logo, which is well known to users.

- **Username**: https://www.pinterest.com/llbean/

- **About You**: Asserting that this is the official pinterest site for L.L. Bean, this area says, "Welcome to the outside. The official Pinterest for L.L.Bean. #BeanOutsider". Their 32 boards focus totally on the outdoor user experience with LL Bean Products.

- **Location**: Freeport Maine.

- **Website**: Here you find a link to the official L.L. Bean website.

One interesting comparison is between L.L. Bean's weddings board and MS's wedding board. The brands clearly delineate themselves visually. L.L. Bean focuses on the outerwear and outdoor activities that wedding goers are experiencing. MS focuses on elegant fashion, flowers, and food. Think carefully about the visual statements you want to make, and never stay away from that focus.

7.4.4 Starting a group board

A group board is a board that several people can share and contribute to. The owner of the account simply need to invite people to add pins to the board by clicking Edit at the bottom of the board and choosing "Who can add pins". Once a user accepts, they can pin anything they want. This system works really well if you have several people on your team who need to supply marketing pins. It also allows you to add colleagues and vendors from outside your team. It's an efficient way to collaborate with everyone who needs to have access to the boards.

Don't be reluctant to add pinners if you need to. Anyone on the team can delete pinners and even block them if you have an issue. You won't be stuck with pinners if they leave or cause a problem.

7.4.5 Creating secret boards

Does the title grab your interest? Secret boards sound so mysterious. They are really a great tool for personal or business use. Secret boards are just what they sound like. They are boards that only you and your chosen friends can see; they aren't public. Imagine the possibilities for you and your collaborators! You can create projects and keep them under wraps. Then you can unveil them when you're ready or keep them permanently secret. How about a board for new product development or perhaps one for personal dream trips you'll take?

Pinterest found out that users liked secret boards when they allowed them to create three secret boards during the 2013 holiday season. After users got the hang of it, they found all sorts of ways to utilize them for holiday shopping lists, secret wish boards, and more. Because of the interest, Pinterest now lets you create up to 500 secret boards at any time. We doubt that you'll have that many secrets, but it's worth a try!

You can create a secret board by following these steps:

1. Log in to Pinterest.
2. Click your name in the upper-right corner
3. Choose your profile and pins
4. Scroll down to the bottom and click the plus sign to create a secret board
5. A window pops up asking to keep it secret - yes or no.

7.5 Developing credibility for your profile

This section explores the types of images that you should consider posting for your business.

Obviously, you want to choose images that are colorful and convey the essence of your brand. Pinterest has several kinds of pins that you can create, as follows:

- **Image pins**: JPGs or videos, which make up the majority of pins you see.

- **Promoted pins**: Pins you pay for.

- **Rich pins**: Allow you to add extra information that makes it easier for customers to find your pins. Use them liberally. You can include pins about movies, recipes, articles, products, and places.

If you want to create a map board, you can select the map option when you are setting up the board. Only the board owner can select the map option, so determine whether you will need it when you set up the board.

You can create as many boards as you need to communicate your message. Don't skimp, and don't worry about whether each one is perfect.

The key aspects of a board are its title and cover picture. These aspects are what the users see first. If the name and picture are straightforward but still enticing, users are likely to at least click to see the board. You have no guarantee that users will stay and perhaps even click other pins, but you want to at least get their attention by making a good first impression. Liken your board to a book cover and title. If your board's title and cover picture aren't immediately intriguing, users won't explore it.

Always encourage your audience to do the following:

- **Repin** your pins to get them circulated.

- **Comment**, because as you know the opinions of friends and colleagues are most valuable.

- **Share and use your hashtags** to let your customer be your best salesperson. Make sure your content is pinnable from your website using widgets.

- **Buy**, which is your favorite customer activity. Make it easy to click the buy button. Evaluate each pin for its usability.

7.6 Narrowing down with guided search

Pinterest wants to make it as easy as possible for you and your customers to find exactly what everyone is looking for. In 2014, the site introduced Pinterest Guided Search for iPhones, iPads, and Android. Guided Search is useful because it lets you to narrow down within a category.

For example, say that your customer is looking for plants for her shaded patio. First she types in shade and gets items including shade garden, shade plants, and shade flowers. She chooses shade plants. Then she is shown additional categories to pick from.

As a marketer, it is important that you conduct these searches for products on mobile devices. You want to know exactly what users will find and how you can make it easy to find your products first.

7.7 Tracking your results

It's easy to assume that your Pinterest traffic is converting customers. But perhaps it's not, and you need to know. You need to analyze what you're doing. Several tools are available to help you see what your customers are doing on Pinterest. These tools include:

- Pinterest's free **built-in analytics dashboard**: You can access this dashboard by first verifying your website and then clicking your account picture in the upper-right corner and choosing Analytics. You can track such items as how many pins are coming from your website in a certain timeframe, what users share most often, and what pins get clicked most.

- **Tailwind**: Tailwind has a free version of this tool that tells you, for example, which pins are being pinned from your website, your number of followers, and the number of re-pins. A professional version is available for a charge.

Chapter 8

Tumblr

8.0 Introduction

Which web-based life has around 456 million sites as of January 2019 and 520 million over a six-month length? If you guessed Tumblr, then, you are absolutely right. In 2014, Tumblr was purchased by Yahoo! for an uncovered 1.1 billion dollars. What started in 2007 as a way for David Karp, Tumblr creator, to easily post media changed into a visual powerhouse with an expansive number of customers.

What makes a Tumblr blog so captivating? It's definitely not hard to use and your image types look remarkable. Tumblr web diaries change from other online life locales since you aren't asked to fuse since quite a while prior, included substance posts. They are proposed to serve the photos that they show, and the interesting thing is bolstered. In this part, we look at what you need to do in any case Tumblr and how to parade your substance to its generally conspicuous advantage.

8.2 Setting Up Shop on Tumblr

Tumblr is free to join and is hosted for you on Tumblr's site. You don't have to worry about getting your own hosting site or paying for a suitable WordPress or other blogging template. This is not insignificant. You probably don't need to hire a developer at the beginning to help you set up your site. However, if you want to customize the template and develop special features that'll help your company, you'll want to consider some assistance.

So, who uses Tumblr? Statistics gives us some interesting demographics about Tumblr users. As of October 2018, about 33% of all desktop users are from the United States, with other 4 countries in the top 5 being the United Kingdom, Brazil, Canada, and Germany, respectively. In the United States alone, 44% of users fall into the 18-24 age bracket and 34% in the 25-34 age bracket.

8.2.1 Creating an account

Like most other social media platforms, creating an account on Tumblr only requires a few easy clicks of a button. All you need to do is think of a distinct URL and blog name that's going to set you and your brand apart. Obviously, you're going to want something that your customers can recognize, remember, and easily go back to. If you're lucky, the name and domain you want won't already be taken by someone else.

Once you have that set up and verified, you're good to go!

8.2.2 Creating the good stuff

You already have a grasp of the initial two things the next is you have to concentrate when putting up a latest platform on your campaigns in social media are the steps below:

1. **How it will become a big help with your customers.**

Are your clients as of now on Tumblr? Make a point to affirm this and see how your clients are utilizing it. On the off chance that you serve a youthful statistic, see to it to join the lively soul of other Tumblr online journals. In the event that your gathering of people fits the statistic however is somewhat more established, don't be hesitant to utilize your blog to flaunt your media. IBM works to the perfection of utilizing Tumblr to convey its message (look at it at (http://ibmblr.tumblr.com), by showing an assortment of classifications.

1. **How it will come along with your strategy.**

Your methodology must be the highlight of all that you do, and you have to lead your Tumblr in a way that incorporates this technique. In the event that a significant amount of share of your clients is not yet on Tumblr in any incredible numbers, you should think about utilizing it to improve your present conveyance — for instance, incorporate connections on your different channels to media on Tumblr.

It's most crucial to keep in mind that your Tumblr blog should not be a duplicate of the content you have on Facebook or Twitter. Tumblr gives you the privilege to include multimedia in a more efficient manner. One of the most useful aspects of having a Tumblr blog is that it forces you to think about more than just text. This is a good thing, since most business blogs are pretty dull and companies don't even realize it. You are challenged to break out the media you own or create something new.

With a Tumblr blog, you have no excuse for posting a few paragraphs and calling it a day. The world of visuals and multimedia is open to you. As a social media marketer, you can make this cornucopia of media choices work to your advantage. You can put up multimedia on Tumblr that's not on your other platforms and then link it. Just don't make your other platforms a "me, too" of Tumblr. Things will not work out for you that way.

To make it easy to select items to curate from your browser, you can also place a Bookmark in the menu. To do this, go to https://www.tumblr.com/app, and drag it onto your browser.

8.2.3 Finding and sharing the good stuff

Tumblr is primarily a community that both creates its own content and shares others'. As a marketer, you're going to want to amass as many followers as you can to get your content shared to as many people as possible. This starts with exploring the platform and all of the content that's related to your brand.

So how do you build your network on Tumblr? Here are a few ideas:

1. **Utilize the hashtags**: Like Twitter and Instagram, Tumblr uses hashtags to categorize its content. Experiment with what hashtags have a lot of related content to your brand. On Tumblr, the more the tags, the merrier! The point is to get more people to see your content, and a lot of people use hashtags to find what interests them.

2. **Reblog whatever is relevant**: You can easily access related posts by clicking on the hashtags and sharing - or, using the appropriate terminology, "reblogging" - what's relevant to you. It also builds a relationship with the user who created the post so if you're reblogging, always give credit to the owner!

3. **Follow, follow, follow**: Exploring the hashtags can also lead you to other users who are posting similar content. Dig around their profile a little more and see if they seem likely to reblog your posts. If you follow them, they're likely to follow you right on back.

4. **Be consistent**: Having a Tumblr profile requires regular upkeep. You're likely to lose followers over time if you're not posting things regularly enough. One of the great features on Tumblr is the ability to schedule posts. You can have a whole lot of posts lined up and the platform will post them for you at the time intervals that you decide on.

8.3 Understanding your Tumblr activity

It is possible to integrate Google Analytics into your Tumblr page so you can track how many users visit your page, as well as other demographics. However, because of the way the Tumblr has structured interaction on their site, there are certain limitations in that, many people may not visit your Tumblr homepage, actually relying instead on what you post that comes up on their Dashboard (similar to the Newsfeed we see on Facebook).

Tumblr has its own built-in activity tracker, which you can view by clicking on the human silhouette on the upper right-hand corner of your browser page. When you look at the activity, it will show you a graph of followers and "notes" over a period of time of your liking. Notes indicate any time that a user interacted with your content by either liking or reblogging it, or both. Unfortunately, the longest time period that you can track your activity over is a month, so partnering this with Google Analytics may still be the most insightful.

Chapter 9

Google+

9.0 Introduction

A couple of years prior, a part covering Google wouldn't have been required in a book via web-based networking media showcasing. But since Google has done as such much in a previous couple of years and has plans to do as such substantially more in the following, a section on Google is without a doubt currently justified.

Google+ propelled in June 2011. Brand pages were added to the platform in November of that year. Google made a social music administration and structured a Google catch for use on different sites and for incorporating different social highlights into Google Search. Apparently, Google's social desire is a lot more noteworthy than its substances today (Google+, for instance, has roughly 540 million clients contrasted with Facebook's billion or more clients), however, that doesn't mean the future may not appear to be unique.

In this part, we'll find how Google has changed from a straightforward web search tool to an internet-based life platform. The point is to have you see how to utilize it further bolstering your good fortune as an advertiser with the rules, tips, and traps.

9.1 Looking at Google's Social Strategy

To realize how to tackle the Google web biological system for online networking showcasing, you have to initially comprehend the center of Google's own social methodology. Generally, Google is as yet an inquiry platform and the most visited webpage on the Internet for both content-based pursuit and video. Most by far of Google's incomes and traffic, originates from Google Search. That is probably not going to change sooner rather than later. Be that as it may, throughout the most recent couple of years, the ascent of Facebook has truly compromised Google's online predominance. An ever-increasing number of individuals look to their companions on platforms, for example, Facebook when they're looking for data, regardless of whether it be item data or eatery suggestions, much of the time even before completing a Google seek. Therefore, Facebook has begun to strip away publicizing dollars that used to go to Google. This has ostensibly made Google anxious.

Google is reacting to this danger in two distinctive ways. To begin with, they've attempted over and again to make interpersonal organizations to rival Facebook, for example, Orkut, which took off just in Brazil and India, and after that Google Buzz, both of which have been shut down. It is fair to say that the Google strategy of creating competing social networks largely failed.

Now, there's Google+, which is designed less as a social network and more as a "social layer," which means that existing

Google applications become more social when they are integrated with Google+. Google has decided to make every other part of the Google ecosystem more social through Google+. Whether it is Google Search or Google Music, Gmail, Google Maps, YouTube, or even Google Apps, they are all getting more and more social through their integration with Google+.

So how does this integration work? The Google+ profiles are used as the background account for many Google services. When you search on Google, you contents shared via Google+ profiles and brand pages. Both of these approaches present unique social media marketing opportunities for marketers.

9.2 Grasping the Google+ Fundamentals

Google+ is another kind of social network for anybody and everybody on the web. Founded in June 2011, on its surface appears to be fundamentally the same as Facebook. Notwithstanding, it does without a doubt have some engineering contrasts that have served to draw in clients to it.

Following are the most crucial features of it:

1. **Google Stream**: This is the landing page that you see when you sign in to Google+. It demonstrates to all of you the posts by individuals in your circles - your associations. Similarly as with Facebook, you can present a message on your stream. The message can be from your own record or a brand page. Be that as it may, even better, after you type the content (or transfer the photo or video), you can pick which circles or which individuals in those circles to impart substance to. In this design, you can firmly oversee who gets the opportunity to perceive what bits of your substance.

2. **Google+ Photos**: Google has put in some pictures that is more squeezed into its web infrastructure. Pressing the Google+ photos icon will bring you to a photo page that is pleasing to the eyes and very useful for everybody. The Google+ Photos philosophy is that the lens from which you view other people's photographs should be the same lens through which

you view the content stream. On the Google+ Photos page, you can choose to view photos in the following categories: photos from your circles, photos from your phone, photos of you, photos from your posts, and your albums (integrating the Google Picasa application).

3. **Google+ Profiles**: Every user on Google+ has a profile page that is similar to the Facebook profile page. All your activity appears on it, including the pages that you may have "+'d" in the past. When you click the +1 button (known as the Google Plus One button) next to some content, you are sharing content with your Google circles. It's similar to the Like button on Facebook. You can select any kind of media (either your own or others') and let people know about it. You can add a photograph, share some information about yourself, upload photographs and videos, and allow others to send you emails and messages from this page. The profile page also shows how many people are in your circles and how many circles you are in.

4. **Google Circles**: Integral to Google+ is the concept of circles, which is the categorization mechanism for people with whom you connect on the platform. They are groups of friends that you organize by topic. Topics can be as straightforward as friends, coworkers, and family, or as rarified as stamp collectors, Justin Bieber fans, and tennis players. On the Circles page, you can add friends to any number of circles. Then when viewing your news feed in Google+, you can

limit the views by particular circles.

As you set yourself up in Google+, create professional circles of people who matter to you and your company. Whether from your personal account or from your Google+ brand page (more on that in the upcoming section "Google brand pages"), you want to create a circle for coworkers, influencers, competitors, and industry analysts. In fact, you could use the same categorization for your circles as your PR team does for its tracking documents. These circles help you keep track of what people are saying. Circles provide you with meaningful opportunities to develop relationships by participating in their conversations.

1. **Google+ Hangouts**: This is probably one of the more unique and fun features of Google+. Hangouts are like virtual rooms that let you run video chats with people who are in your circles. It is a focused video chat with friends, family, coworkers, or business contacts. Because Hangouts are triggered through circles; it is easy to find the group you want to talk to and then to set up a Google Hangout.

You can use Google Hangouts to have business conversations with other people in your company or even suppliers, business partners, or customers. If your brand is on Google+, Hangouts are a great way to socialize with customers or to run online events with them. For example, you can announce products on Google Hangouts and invite all your customers, business partners, suppliers, and employees to participate. Hangouts On-Air are particularly interesting because they give users the ability to create instant webcasts over Google+. These broadcasts can also be recorded for retrieval at a future date.

1. **Google+ Huddles**: Huddles, another valuable feature of Google+, enables you to run group messaging with people in a given circle. So just as Hangouts lets you run live video chat sessions with them, Huddles allows you to talk to them via group messaging. Google Huddles is currently available only for the iPhone and Android devices. You cannot access it from a web browser. Arguably, this tool has no direct implications for marketers as yet, but it is a useful collaboration tool among marketers within an organization.

9.3 Google Brand Pages

These pages are similar to the user pages on Google+ and include features such as Circles, streams, Hangouts, and Huddles, but they also have some key differences from those pages. The differences are designed to allow for the nuances of social media marketing as well as to prevent brands from over-marketing on the social media platform.

Following are the key differences with Google+ brand pages and what they mean for you:

- **Adding users to circles requires permission.**

A Google+ brand page cannot add a user to a circle unless that user has already added the page to one of his circles. This is very important because it prevents a brand from sending you messages until you have explicitly added the brand page to one of your circles and are open to receiving content from that brand. In other words, brands have to earn their place in a user's stream before they can start pushing messages into it.

- **Content is public.**

In contrast to personal profiles, pages on Google+ are set to public by default. This means that not only can the people who have the brand in a circle view the content, but anyone who visits the page can, too. Most brands want more people to see their content, so this default setting serves everyone well. It also gives individuals an opportunity to scan the content being published by the brand before choosing to add the page to one of his or her own circles. The default setting can be changed by the brand administrator.

- **Pages have +1 and Add to Circles buttons.**

Individual user pages have only the Add to Circles button in the top-right corner. Brand pages allow you to +1 the page or add content to it as well. The +1 button is something that Google is trying to push out across the entire Internet. When you +1 a piece of content, it improves that content's rankings in the Google search engine. And when you +1 a page on Google+, it brings about the same result as when you do so on an external website. This is a seemingly small feature but a very important one.

- **It is integrated with Search.**

Google is working hard to integrate Google+ with Google Search. If you search for a brand and add the plus sign (+) in the search box before the name of the brand, in the search results you'll be given the opportunity to add the page to a circle immediately. In fact, some users are taken directly to the Google+ brand page.

9.4 Tips and Tricks For Google+

Although Google+ may appear to be extremely large with 540 million users, many of those users do not use Google+ as a social network but just as a way to log in to Google services. We have yet to see how the platform will evolve and become really valuable for marketers. Only time will tell.

However, here are some tips and tricks to consider so that you are prepared for the many enhancements to Google+ that we know are coming:

1. **Set up shop on Google+ now.**

There's no question that the brands who set up shop early on Google+ are the ones who are able to attract the most people to their brands on the platform. This was the case with Facebook in its early days (some of the largest pages are still the oldest ones). The same applies to Google. In fact, we've already seen that the brands that were part of the Google+ launch already have significantly more people in their circles than the brands that joined later.

1. **"Write once, publish everywhere" doesn't work.**

Before you start publishing extensively on Google+, take the time to familiarize yourself with the platform and how individuals are using it. You'll notice that it is often used as a medium for more serious conversations. Although this may change in time, the threaded nature of conversations still remain with a more professional tone. As a result, don't automatically republish content designed for Facebook on Google+. You could, of course, repurpose the content and make it more suitable for the tone surrounding Google+

1.   Focus on search engine optimization.

One of the hidden benefits of participating as a brand on Google+ is the search engine optimization advantages that come with it. Google+ is not a stand-alone social network. It is part of a broader Google ecosystem that has information discovery at its core. As a result, every link you post on Google+ as a brand that's then clicked as a +1 on Google+ gets better optimized for search engines. That alone is a compelling reason to be an early participant on Google+.

1.   The +1 that you see in Google+ requires attention.

Not only do the +1 button clicks impact search engine results, but in time, they will also have a direct influence on paid search and display ads running on Google. If Google has its way, these buttons will be as pervasive across the Internet as the Facebook Like buttons. This means that when you redesign your website, you'll want to include those Google+ buttons. And even though having a brand page may not directly drive the increased usage of the button (that is, make your content and your brand be clicked as a +1 a lot more), having the community can certainly serve as a strong foundation.

9.5 Learning from the examples of others

The best way to learn what to do and what not to do on Google+ is to pay attention to what other brands are doing. See how often they post, what they post, and how their content sharing on Google+ jives with their Facebook strategies. Pay attention to user activity on their pages.

9.6 Listening to Google and Music

Just lately Google have founded a new feature in which it can compete with more well-known brands like iTunes on all kinds of devices. It is very crucial for Google to implement this so that their Android platform will not get left behind by Apple. In this section, we will discuss about the core service of it and its other features that will greatly help you in your social media marketing.

The Google Music has the following features:

- **You can upload all your songs to its platform.**

It can contain up to 20,000 songs without any fees at all. However, if you have a massive amount of songs, it can take a lot of time for it to be uploaded.

- **The songs can be utilized in various ways.**

You can manage your music on an Android device or through https://music.google.com/music/, too.

- **You can get a lot of song suggestions from it**

These suggestions are originated on what you possessed currently in the locker and the level of frequency you prefer. It also lets you purchase songs that will be on all platforms once you purchased them.

- **All the music that you buy in the Google Android Market can be shared.**

The most sought part of the Google Music platform is the feature of dissemination that you can enable. The way it works is simple: when you buy some music, you can choose to share it with your Google+ circles. After you've chosen which circles to share it with, your purchased content appears in their Google+ streams, where they can listen to the tracks for free (one listen per track). You can imagine that as the core Google+ functionality improves, the ways in which Google+ integrates with it also increase.

What does Google's entrance into social platforms mean for social media marketing? Just think about the possibilities for a moment. As a brand, you can not only share content with certain members of your customer base (through specific circles), but also potentially start sharing specific music. If you're a brand that plays in pop culture and for whose customers' music matters, this could be a really interesting way to attract attention to your brand and build loyalty around it. Needless to say, doing this right means doing it in a way that makes sense for your brand and for your customers.

Conclusion

When people start talking online, building relationships and meeting new people through people they already know, the simplest form of online networking begins. Just like the old word of mouth, inviting your friends who then invite their friend leads to an extensive networking circle. And with this came the social media expansion.

There is a difference between social networking and social media that needs to be made clear. Social networking is creating a web of connections between you and friends on sites such as Facebook, Twitter, LinkedIn, etc. Social media, on the other hand, is the content that you distribute. So it's about your content on blogs and all social sites. If you were to think about this in terms of coffee, the coffee cup or mug is the network. What you drink in it is the social media. If you decide to be, say, a cappuccino person or a latte person, would be up to you. In the same way online, you would do this by choosing your cup or network, which could be Facebook, LinkedIn, or any others. Then you decide what social media content (videos, pictures, text, etc) you will put inside it when you post, tweet, blog, or the like.

Although social media marketing seems to be fresh and new, it has been around for decades and actually goes back to the early days of computers and the internet. It may have been outdated and almost archaic before the world wide web (www) really took off with mass appeal, but it was still a method for online communication since the beginning of computers. Not so long ago, Friendster, MySpace, and Tribe, were coined as the innovative new sites until the likes of Facebook came along almost by accident. Founder of Facebook, Mark Zuckerberg, started his social network as a communication tool much like those before him, and he did so within his college campus to help students manage their social lives online. Hoffman, behind LinkedIn, seemingly suddenly emerged as well as one of the world's largest social networks. Most social sites started with different types of user-generated content, photo sharing, poking, and blogs among friends. But today, the Newsfeeds we see allow people to find out what is happening in their friends' circles, their businesses, and among colleagues' lives. All of this resulted in the biggest compilation of sharing information the world could imagine.

With new sites springing up all the time, millions of people are now able to turn to social networking sites every day to communicate with groups of people around them - in a sense of their community - about anything from informal announcements to important business news. Social media is a new modern media stream, aimed at social interaction with a selected target audience. Fantastic publishing tools give you the ability to reach friends and acquaintances through monologue type conversations which turn into dialogues amongst your fans and followers. More and more people are using social media to communicate. Different people use social media networks for different things. Some use it for PR, marketing, and broadcasting their business message to achieve a viral effort for a concept. Others use it for socialising and interaction within a community. Even freelancers, authors, and celebrities use social media networks to socialise with their fans. This goes to show the wide scope of social media and what it has to offer to you.

Traditionally, networking is about offering advice, doing favors and generally building business relationships which can be done online or offline. It can be a great way to promote your business and brand, and it offers a way to reach people who might otherwise be very difficult to engage by conventional sales methods. This progresses to a sense of personal relationships and potential clients.

With the deep dive, guidelines, and tips presented in this book for the top social media platforms available today, it's time for you to get started on your own social media marketing campaign. Good luck to you as you start the journey!

---

[1] Prices are as of January 2019 and may be subject to change.

[2] Prices are as of January 2019 and are subject to change.